# THE MIRROR

# THE MIRROR

*A Play in Two Acts*

ISAAC BASHEVIS SINGER
*Edited by David Stromberg*

# ACT I

# SCENE 1

*A huge mirror from which the glass can be removed. Only the ornate frame is left, facing the audience.*

Zirel    *Partially facing mirror.* So. *She looks around, removes her headcovering, brushes her hair. To her image in the mirror she says:* Not a word. *Puts her finger across her lips to indicate silence. Steps are heard. Zirel quickly replaces the covering on her head as Yenta enters.*

Yenta    Looking at herself in the mirror … We're expecting guests!

Zirel    Who comes to Krashnik? Such a God for-saken village.

Yenta    My grandmother used to say, "When some-one passes through Krashnik in a cart, the wheels haven't yet entered the town, but the horse's head is already gone."

Zirel    A clever old lady.

Yenta    My uncle Leibush used to say, "Adam did not urinate in Kranshik and that's the reason God has forgotten it."

| | |
|---|---|
| Zirel | Watch your language! But it's the truth. This is a hole, not a place. It's so quiet here that there's a constant ringing in my ears. |
| Yenta | This evening the young women will gather at Shiffra's to chop cabbage. Perhaps the mistress will go? Shiffra invited you. |
| Zirel | No, Yenta. I can't stand their silly talk. They babble all evening long about last year's cholent, or about a baby's diarrhea. I'd rather be alone. |
| Yenta | What would the mistress and the young master like for dinner tomorrow evening? |
| Zirel | Tomorrow's dinner – who can think about food when we don't even do anything? And what are the options anyway? Again noodle soup, again carrot stew. It's not your fault, Yenta, but even the meals are coming out of my ears. |
| Yenta | The butchers bought an ox, but they haven't slaughtered it yet. |
| Zirel | You don't expect me to eat a live ox!? Besides, why do you ask me about the master's food? He keeps fasting. |
| Yenta | There's a saying that The Torah satisfies. |
| Zirel | The Torah wouldn't satisfy me. |
| Yenta | While we're waiting for the ox to be slaughtered, should I take the spotted hen out to be killed? |
| Zirel | Why is it the hen's fault? |
| Yenta | Perhaps I should cook rice instead of noodles for the broth? |

| | |
|---|---|
| Zirel | Let it be rice. |
| Yenta | The old master, your father, brought me a gift from Danzig. |
| Zirel | Really? What did he bring? |
| Yenta | *Showing her necklace.* This coral necklace. |
| Zirel | Oh, I didn't notice it. It's beautiful. |
| Yenta | What did he bring you? |
| Zirel | I haven't opened the box yet. |
| Yenta | You haven't? Whenever your father goes away, I lie awake at night thinking of what he'll bring me. |
| Zirel | Whatever he brings is never useful here. There isn't anyone to get dressed up for, except perhaps the demons. |
| Yenta | Oh, the mistress shouldn't utter such words, especially in the evening. *She spits three times.* |
| Zirel | Even respectable demons wouldn't stick their noses in here. |
| Yenta | Please, mistress, don't mention them. You utter a word and it becomes true. Some time ago a woman in Izhbitza said to her daughter-in-law, "go and fetch me a pail of water from the well, but don't fall in." She left carrying the pail and never returned. Her mother-in-law went to look for her and found her in the well with her head down and her feet up. Dead! |
| Zirel | All kinds of misfortunes happen in these miserable villages. |
| Yenta | I have dreams as terrifying as the wild forests. The moment I close my eyes, I'm |

attacked by beasts. I sink into a swamp and can't free myself. The sky is full of fire and a chimney sweep with blazing eyes flies down. His broom is made of living snakes.

Zirel    Perhaps you don't recite the Shema before you go to sleep.

Yenta    I recite.

Zirel    Why aren't *you* engaged yet?

Yenta    Matches are proposed, but either he's a baker or a coachman. After having served in a cultured home so many years, I can no longer stand these brutes.

Zirel    What would you want? A Yeshiva boy like my husband?

Yenta    I don't mind a widower, but he should be a fine person, not a common lout. All they want is a belly full of cabbage and a house full of children.

Zirel    Better than an empty house.

Yenta    The mistress is still young. Where there's a husband, there's always hope.

*Yenta exits*

Zirel    She's a victim too! Well, I'll read the story-book. *Reads.* Once there was a sultan and he had four young wives. One was a brunette, one a redhead, one was blonde and one had hair like spun gold that reached to her knees. They all could sing, play and dance.

At night the Sultan used to sit on his throne and his wives sang and danced for him. They had little bells on their knuckles and when they danced, the bells tinkled. While the Sultan smoked his narghillah and pursued his own thoughts—

*The door opens and Abraham Frampoler enters*

| | |
|---|---|
| Abraham | Daughter, why are you sitting at the mirror? |
| Zirel | Where should I sit? |
| Abraham | A Jewish daughter is not permitted to spend so much time looking into a mirror. |
| Zirel | What is a Jewish daughter permitted to do? |
| Abraham | Recite Psalms, take care of the household, look into a Holy Book. Last time I brought you *The Rod of Punishment.* Did you read it? |
| Zirel | Yes, I read it. There are seven gehennas and each one is sixty times hotter than the one before. Their names? *Sheol, Avadon, Tsalmavet*—I forget the other four. |
| Abraham | The names are not important, but a person's deeds are. The Book of Remembrance is open. It reads by itself and every person inscribes his own sins on its pages. |

| | |
|---|---|
| Zirel | What sins can one commit in Krashnik? |
| Abraham | What are you saying, daughter?! One is punished for every careless word, even for a sinful thought. As for gossip and lies, retribution is terrible. Tell me, dear, are you careful about your ablutions? |
| Zirel | I'm careful. |
| Abraham | Are you counting the days? |
| Zirel | I'm counting the days, the nights, the hours, event the minutes. Besides, the bath attendant keeps track of these things. If you so much as yawn in Krashnik, the whole village yawns with you. *She yawns.* |
| Abraham | How did you like my gift? |
| Zirel | I haven't opened it yet. |
| Abraha, | You mother, peace be with her, when I brought her a gift, she immediately broke the ribbon with her teeth. She had strong teeth until the end. |
| Zirel | How did her teeth help her? *Opens a drawer, removes a box, and breaks the ribbon with her teeth.* Amber beads. |
| Abraham | Yes, amber. The very best you can get in Danzig. |
| Zirel | *She puts them around her neck and looks into the mirror.* Oh, how beautiful! *With hesitation.* May I kiss you? |
| Abraham | Kiss? Me? |

| | |
|---|---|
| Zirel | You are my father, not a stranger. |
| Abraham | It's not right. |
| Zirel | There isn't even anyone to kiss in Krashnik. |
| Abraham | Maybe I shouldn't say this, but you have a husband. |
| Zirel | All I have is a marriage contract. |
| Abraham | Does he come to you? |
| Zirel | He comes. |
| Abraham | In the night, after the ablutions? |
| Zirel | Yes, after the ablutions. |
| Abraham | And on other nights? |
| Zirel | Sometimes. |
| Abraham | How often? |
| Zirel | Not often. |
| Abraham | A Jewish daughter should be modest, but nevertheless she should try to attract her husband with pretty clothes, jewelry, and nice words. |
| Zirel | Does he hear what I say to him? He's either praying, or studying, or just murmuring. |
| Abraham | Even at night in bed? |
| Zirel | He buzzes like a bee. |
| Abraham | He most probably recites the Zohar by heart. I've warned him not to indulge in the Kabbalah. One should not study these mysteries before the age of thirty. The Mishnah tells us that of the four Tanaites who gazed into the Orchard |

|          | of Creation, only one emerged unscathed. |
|----------|-------------------------------------------|
| Zirel    | Father, since you mention it, I must tell you the truth. Even when Shloimele approaches me, he only talks about such matters. |
| Abraham  | What matters? |
| Zirel    | God, Angels. He wants to bring the Messiah. |
| Abraham  | At his age? It's completely wrong. |
| Zirel    | He eats next to nothing. He asked me not to tell you, but all week long he doesn't touch meat. Even bread he tastes only enough to be able to say the blessings. |
| Abraham  | It's wrong. If one doesn't eat, one doesn't have any strength. |
| Zirel    | Perhaps we should leave this God-forsaken place. |
| Abraham  | What kind of talk is this? God forsakes no place. Besides, I have my house here, my business, my forest, my workers. If I move, everything will go to pieces. |
| Zirel    | I can't stand it any more. There's no one to talk to. As long as mother was alive, I didn't feel it so deeply. Since she passed, I'm completely alone. |
| Abraham  | I understand you, daughter. And how I understand you! Matchmakers are after me, but since your mother died, |

all women look like geese. They're all so ordinary. They speak so loudly, without any sense of taste. In Danzig, they introduced me to three women, one after another. I conversed with them and got nauseous.

| | |
|---|---|
| Zirel | What will become of us, father? |
| Abraham | Only God can help us. |
| Zirel | I keep thinking about divorce. |
| Abraham | Divorce Shloimele? He's an orphan and a descendant of righteous saints. To cause him any grief would be playing with fire. |
| Zirel | He isn't a man! |
| Abraham | What is he, a woman? I will have a good talk with him. Things can be corrected. Life itself is a series of corrections. What you spoil today, you must correct tomorrow. |
| Zirel | Father, this cannot be corrected. |
| Abraham | One must try. I will talk to him. |
| Zirel | There is a saying that you can't get pregnant from words alone. |
| Abraham | Such loose talk! *He slaps her.* |
| Zirel | You can slap me, father, but this will not change things. |
| Abraham | Forgive me, but your words make me jump out of my skin. |
| Zirel | Jump back into it. Everything will be as it was. |

| | |
|---|---|
| Abraham | That a daughter of mine should express herself in such a shameless way! *Exits.* |
| Zirel | It's not the world. It's me that's coming to an end. *Long pause. She opens her housecoat and stares at the nipple of her left breast, then resumes reading the book.* "Once, a messenger came to the sultan from the Isle of Madagascar and told him that one of his concubines had … " *She lifts her eyes and sees a demon.* My, how ugly you are! |
| Demon | My, how beautiful you are! |
| Zirel | *Long pause.* Who are you? |
| Demon | Fear not, I'm an imp, not a demon. My fingers have no nails, my mouth has no teeth, my arms stretch like licorice, my horns are as pliable as wax. My power lies in my tongue. I'm a fool by trade and I have come to cheer you up because you are alone. |
| Zirel | Where were you before? |
| Demon | In the bedroom, behind the stove, where the cricket chirps and the mouse rustles, between a dried wreath and a faded willow branch. |
| Zirel | What did you do there? |
| Demon | I looked at you. |
| Zirel | Since when? |
| Demon | Since your wedding night. |
| Zirel | What did you eat? |

| | |
|---|---|
| Demon | The fragrance of your body, the glow of your hair, the light of your eyes, the sadness of your face. |
| Zirel | You flatterer! Who are you? What is your mission? |
| Demon | My father was a goldsmith and my mother a succubus. They copulated in a cellar on a bundle of rotting straw and I was their bastard. |
| Zirel | Where did all this happen? Here in Krashnik? |
| Demon | For a time we lived in a settlement of devils on Mt. Seir. But when they found out that my father was a human, we were driven out. I've been without a home since. The devils avoid me because I remind them of the sons of Adam. The daughters of Eve see Satan in me. Dogs bark at me, children weep when they See me. Why are they afraid? I've harmed no one. My only desire is to gaze at beautiful women—to gaze and converse with them. |
| Zirel | Why converse? The beautiful aren't always wise. |
| Demon | In Paradise, the wise are the footstools of the beautiful. |
| Zirel | My book taught me otherwise. |
| Demon | What do these books know? The people who write them have brains like fleas. |

|  | They parrot each other. Ask me when you want to know something. Wisdom extends only to the first heaven. From there on everything is lust. |
|---|---|
| Zirel | Lust in heaven? I don't believe it. |
| Demon | Don't you know that the angels are headless? The Seraphim play in the sand like children. The Cherubim can't count. The Aralim chew their cud before the Throne of Glory. |
| Zirel | How about God? |
| Demon | God plays around. He spends his time pulling Leviathan by the tail and being licked by the wild ox. Or else he tickles the *Shekhinah*, making her lay myriads of eggs, and each egg is a star. |
| Zirel | Now I know you're making fun of me. |
| Demon | If I do, may a funny bone grow on my nose. It's a long time since I squandered my quota of lies. |
| Zirel | Can you beget children? |
| Demon | Like a mule, I'm the last of the line. But this does not blunt my desire, especially for those are married and beautiful— |
| Zirel | *Bursts out laughing.* My mother didn't bring me up to be a devil's lover. Away with you, or I'll have you exorcised. |
| Demon | Why bother? *Auf Wiedersehen.* |
| Zirel | Wait a second. *She enumerates.* I have a husband, a father. I have gold, silver, |

|        | capes, furs. My shoes have the highest heels in the whole of Krashnik. |
|--------|------------------------------------------------------------------------|
| Demon  | Yes or no?                                                              |
| Zirel  | No.                                                                     |
| Demon  | No is no. *He fades away*                                               |

*Curtain*

# Scene 2

*Zirel sits at a small table on which there's an ornate storybook and a morality book.*

Zirel    *She reads from the morality book.* What are the pleasures of this world? Nothing but vanity. When the time comes for man to die, his body becomes like a torn garment. If he sinned against the Creator, each sin becomes an evil spirit, and these spirits attack him, torture him, pull him in all directions. And because he's a corpse, he cannot resist them and his torment is great. *Pause.* As a matter of fact, the torment is great right now. *Slams the morality book shut and opens the storybook in the middle, reading.* And after Zlichah the Witch had waited seven days and seven nights, and Ketev Merreri did not show up, she lit two wax candles, went into the dark forest, and uttered a spell:

> Swift is the wind,
> Deep the ditch,
> Sleek the black cat,

Come within reach.
Strong is the lion,
Dumb is the fish,
Reach from the silence,
And take your dish.

And when Ketev Merreri heard this spell he came riding on a hoop, his hair loose, his nose red as fire. He had a retinue of demons riding after him: One on a broom, one on a stick, one on a hedgehog and one on a snake. One sang and one danced. One performed somersaults and the other jumped over his own tail. And when Zlichah the Witch saw Ketev Merreri, she fell at his feet, calling, "Take me, my love, and do with me as you please." *Pause.*

*Shloimele is at the door.*

| | |
|---|---|
| Shloimele | Good evening. |
| Zirel | Hello. |
| Shloimele | Did you say something? |
| Zirel | I said nothing. |
| Shloimele | I thought I heard a voice, or voices. |
| Zirel | You imagined it. |
| Shloimele | Whenever I come in, you're alone. This isn't good. |
| Zirel | Who else should be here? |
| Shloimele | You should go visit a neighbor. |

| | |
|---|---|
| Zirel | I have no one to go to. You have a study house. You are busy with the Torah. There's no study house for women, and the Torah is forbidden to us. |
| Shloimele | It's because our sages wanted the female to take care of the household and the children. |
| Zirel | We have no children. |
| Shloimele | One should never be resigned. As you sit here sunk in melancholy, great things are happening in the world. |
| Zirel | What are they? |
| Shloimele | Are you able to keep a secret? |
| Zirel | I keep many secrets. |
| Shloimele | The Messiah is coming any day! |
| Zirel | Again? How do you know? |
| Shloimele | I know. Satan has raised a great accusation, but the powers interceded for us and we have prevailed. The Messiah is already in Rome! |
| Zirel | Why in Rome? |
| Shloimele | This is what the Talmud has predicted. He will sit at the gates of Rome and bandage his wounds. Then Elijah will blow the ram's horn and his declaration will be heard in all the lands: Redemption has come to the world! |
| Zirel | And what will happen then? |
| Shloimele | A cloud will descend and take all the Jews to the Holy Land. A fiery temple will come down from the heavens and |

|           | land in Jerusalem. Then there will be the resurrection of the dead— |
| Zirel     | Will mother rise from her grave? |
| Shloimele | Mothers, fathers, grandfathers, grandmothers. About this event the psalmist has predicted: "Then our mouths will be filled with laughter." A young man of twenty will have a grandson of eighty. *He laughs.* |
| Zirel     | How do you know all this? |
| Shloimele | If you will give me your holy promise not to reveal it, I will tell it to you, but it's a sacred trust. If you should, God forbid, tell it to anyone, you will destroy the universe. |
| Zirel     | Unless I decide to destroy the universe I will keep my mouth shut. |
| Shloimele | Elijah appeared to me! |
| Zirel     | When? |
| Shloimele | The other night I lay in bed and the room was all dark. Suddenly, it was as light as day. What am I saying? Not like the shining of the sun, but the brilliance of a thousand suns. |
| Zirel     | I was in the bedroom, too, but I didn't see anything. |
| Shloimele | Only to those who study the Kabbalah are these mysteries revealed. It was certainly not because of my merit, but the merit of my holy ancestors. God's face was hidden for a long time. Satan |

and the Evil Spirit endeavored to make evil permanent, but the Kabbaklists in Safed gathered in caves and combined the sacred letters of God's many names—

| | |
|---|---|
| Zirel | When will he actually come? |
| Shloimele | No one knows the exact day. It may be tomorrow and it could be the day after tomorrow. Once the Messiah comes, free choice will end. Use it while there's still time. |
| Zirel | What should I do? |
| Shloimele | Recite the Psalms, give charity. This is the highest virtue. |
| Zirel | Krashnik no longer has paupers. The old ones died and the young ones left for Lublin. |
| Shloimele | A single good deed can tip the scale. |
| Zirel | Will we remain husband and wife after the Messiah comes? |
| Shloimele | Yes, but the bodies will slowly fade away, and only the souls will remain. |
| Zirel | And what will the souls do? |
| Shloimele | Study the Torah. |
| Zirel | Me too? |
| Shloimele | Women will be allowed to learn too. We will study together. |
| Zirel | You know so much and I know nothing. |
| Shloimele | Once the body is gone, there is no real difference between male and female. |

| | |
|---|---|
| Zirel | And how will I be your wife? |
| Shloimele | I will reveal mysteries to you and you will receive them. The male is the giver and the female os the receiver. |
| Zirel | Will we have children? |
| Shloimele | The saints will discover new meanings in the Torah and these commentaries will be their children. |
| Zirel | No eating? |
| Shloimele | Souls don't eat. |
| Zirel | How about sleep? |
| Shloimele | Souls don't sleep. |
| Zirel | Will they constantly study the Torah? |
| Shloimele | Constantly. |
| Zirel | In that case it will be more or less like it is here in Krashnik today. |
| Shloimele | What are you saying? The joy of the Torah is greater than all the pleasures of the world. |
| Zirel | There won't be any love? |
| Sloimele | One must love only the Creator. |
| Zirel | So you admit that you don't love me. |
| Shloimele | I do, but since God created you, the love belongs to him. |
| Zirel | Before the Messiah comes, kiss me. |
| Shloimele | This is sinful chatter. |
| Zirel | I've performed my ablutions. |
| Shloimele | Just now, when all the worlds are trembling and everything hangs on a hair, you want to commit such follies. |

| | |
|---|---|
| Zirel | I don't believe a word you say. You've been talking about the Messiah since the day we married, |
| Shloimele | *He puts his hands over his ears.* I don't want to hear this. |
| Zirel | Take your hands away. *She tries to tear his hands from his ears.* What I really want is a divorce, not your kisses. Divorce me. You're not a man! |
| Shloimele | You wicked woman. |
| Zirel | *Clutching his sidelocks.* Swear that you'll divorce me. |
| Shloimele | One is not allowed to swear. What do you want from me? Father— |
| Zirel | Don't bring in your dead father, and don't tell me that you're an orphan. I, too, am an orphan. Will you divorce me or not? |
| Shloimele | Zirel, Zirel, why do you torture me? |

*The door opens and Yenta sticks her head in.*

| | |
|---|---|
| Zirel | *Angrily.* What is it? |
| Yenta | They've already slaughtered the ox. |
| Zirel | They slaughtered him? Good for him. His ordeal is over. |
| Shloimele | When the redemption comes, there will be no slaughter. |
| Zirel | There will be. As long as there will be knives, there will be slaughter. |

| | |
|---|---|
| Yenta | I'll ask for ten pounds of flanken. Should I also buy a foot? |
| Zirel | A foot, a head. Whatever you want. |
| Shloimele | Well, I'll go. *He exits.* |
| Yenta | I had the spotted hen killed. We'll make soup out of her. |
| Zirel | The Messiah is coming and she's making soup! Go, Yenta, leave me alone. |
| Yenta | Please forgive me, mistress. *She exits.* |
| *Zirel* | *A long pause and then she again approaches the mirror and recites.* |

Swift is the wind,
Deep the ditch,
Sleek the black cat,
Come within reach.
Strong is the lion,
Dumb the fish,
Reach from the silence,
And take your dish.

*She stares into the mirror but no one appears.*

| | |
|---|---|
| Zirel | God, why did you create the world? You must have been as lonely as I am. You suffered countless ages and then decided to bring some joy into your eternal existence. Heaven doesn't seem much happier than Krashnik. |

*The demon appears in the mirror.*

| | |
|---|---|
| Zirel | Here he is. |
| Demon | Why do you speak to God? He doesn't hear you. |
| Zirel | Doesn't he exist? |
| Demon | He's old and tired. He worked six days to create this little earth and then he went to rest. He's been resting since. |
| Zirel | And who rules the universe? |
| Demon | Asmodeus, our Lord. |
| Zirel | You've grown. The last time I saw you, you were nothing but an imp. Does your kind grow so quickly? |
| Demon | Corn grows from rain and we grow from pleasure. |
| Zirel | You mean wickedness? |
| Demon | Call it what you like. |
| Zirel | Where were you? |
| Demon | In the poor old shtetls: Turbin, Frampol, Bilgoray. |
| Zirel | And what did you do? |
| Demon | What can one do in Frampol? Little things. I whistled down chimneys and danced in the public bath. I overturned a pot of cholent in a poor man's kitchen. I made a woman unclean when her husband returned from a trip. To do big things, a demon needs a mate. |
| Zirel | Can't you find one among your own? |
| Demon | After knowing you, Zirel, all other females are like geese to me. |
| Zirel | What do you see in me? |

| | |
|---|---|
| Demon | To see your charm, you'd need to have my eyes. |
| Zirel | All I know is that I'm sad. |
| Demon | All your sadness could turn into joy in one night. |
| Zirel | What kind of joy? |
| Demon | We both have the same passion: to play. |
| Zirel | Play what? |
| Demon | We could travel together to Lublin, to Warsaw, to the Congealed Sea. We could fly like birds to the Dead Sea and to the ruins of Sodom. |
| Zirel | What about work? |
| Demon | In the whole of creation there is only one species that works: man. |
| Zirel | I read in *The Inheritance of the Deer* that all demons are faithless. You'd betray me. |
| Demon | Men betray. Demons share. |
| Zirel | If I love someone, I don't want to share him with any one. |
| Demons | Human folly. Asmodeus, our king, is mightier than God. He loves his wife Lilith more than anything in the universe. But one night a year, on the winter solstice, he shares her with the twelve Lords of the netherworld. It's our most joyful night, and when she returns to him at dawn, they love one another more than ever. |

| | |
|---|---|
| Zirel | And what is he doing while she lies with the twelve Lords? |
| Demon | He lies with their twelve wives. |
| Zirel | And there's no punishment for such behavior? |
| Demon | Punishment is a human invention. |
| Zirel | I will not follow you. But what do you want me to do? |
| Demon | Come into the mirror. |
| Zirel | How can one enter a mirror? It's flat. |
| Demon | Don't you see its depth? |
| Zirel | It's all imagination. |
| Demon | Enter imagination. |
| Zirel | I don't know your name. |
| Demon | Hurmizah. Hurmizah, son of Onan. |
| Zirel | Away with you, Hurmizah, to where the heavens are copper and the earth iron—where men do not work and cattle do not tread. |
| Demon | Is this your last word? |
| Zirel | My very last. |
| Demon | In that case I swear by Asmodeus's beard that you will never see my face again. |
| Zirel | I swear I will not call you again. |
| Demon | You will yearn for me just the same. |
| Zirel | I will yearn but not for you. |
| Demon | If you prefer your Shloimele, you can have him. |
| Zirel | Away from here or I will sprinkle salt on your tail. |

| | |
|---|---|
| Demon | I'm going, but there is no one to take my place. *Whistles. Exits.* |
| Zirel | What does he want from me? Oh mother, help me. *Covers her face.* |

*Curtain*

# SCENE 3

*A*braham *speaking to Shloimele.*

| | |
|---|---|
| Abraham | This is not the right way, Shloimele. |
| Shloimele | The night is darkest before dawn. |
| Abraham | We cannot force the End of Days. Without patience, we would have perished in exile long ago. |
| Shloimele | How much longer will we suffer? So much poverty, so much sickness. Krashnik is a tiny village, but the Angle of Death is always here. All night long, black dogs bark. Every day there's a burial. The poorhouse is full of sick people. The kings wage bitter wars, Jews are beaten all over the world. |
| Abraham | This is how it was for God knows how long. |
| Shloimele | There must be a way to bring the Messiah. If he does not come soon, there will be no one left for him to come to. |

| | |
|---|---|
| Abraham | You cannot dictate to the Almighty. *Pause.* My daughter complains about you. |
| Shloimele | What am I doing to her? |
| Abraham | A man must spend some time with his wife. Even the saints did not ignore their wives. The Torah tells us that when Abimelech looked out of the window, he saw Isaac playing with his wife, Rebeccah, and Rashi explains that they were copulating. |
| Shloimele | Could Isaac, our patriarch, have copulated with his wife in broad daylight, outside of Abimelech's window? |
| Abraham | The Torah always means what it says. The body makes its demands. A man should come to his wife in her pure days. |
| Shloimele | I come to her. |
| Abraham | One should talk to her. |
| Shloimele | I talk to her. I tell her about the saints, but she always interrupts me with vanity and nonsense. |
| Abraham | In bed, even this is allowed. My Temerl, peace be with her, was a devout woman, but she liked to play with me. This is the reason I cannot replace her. |
| Shloimele | *Puts his hands over his ears.* I don't want to hear. |
| Abraham | Zirel is Temerl's daughter. You cannot put her off just with holy writings. If you |

|           | wanted to be a hermit, you shouldn't have married. |
|-----------|----------------------------------------------------|
| Shloimele | I wanted to fulfill the commandment: Thou shalt be fruitful and multiply. |
| Abraham   | When a woman has no desire for her husband, she does not conceive. |
| Shloimele | Father-in-law, what shall I do? |
| Abraham   | Kiss her, caress her. Remind her that you love her. Tell her a joke. |
| Shloimele | Make light of things? |
| Abraham   | Even holy men sometimes play around. |
| Shloimele | The ancients could do anything. They were great. If they were Angles, we are only men, and if they were men, we are donkeys. This is what the Talmud says. |
| Abraham   | It isn't good. Zirel's anguish is mine. |
| Shloimele | I will pray for her. |
| Abraham   | I'm afraid that you were bewitched. The Jew of Babylon will soon visit Krashnik. He specialized in removing spells from young couples. |
| Shloimele | One is not permitted to have dealings with such men. They are warlocks. They serve Satan. |
| Abraham   | Witchcraft can only be cured by witchcraft. |
| Shloimele | Father-in-law, I won't have anything to do with him. |
| Abraham   | In that case you will have to divorce my daughter. |
| Shloimele | I'm leaving now! |

| | |
|---|---|
| Abraham | Where are you going? |
| Shloimele | To the ritual bath. |
| Abraham | Again to the ritual bath? |
| Shloimele | After such talk, one has to be cleansed. |

*The door opens and Yenta enters carrying a long broom.*

| | |
|---|---|
| Yenta | Oy, forgive me, master. I thought the room was empty and I came in to clean it. |
| Abraham | Don't run away. Shloimele is going to the ritual bath. Give him a shirt and a pair of drawers. |
| Yenta | Why? It isn't Friday. |
| Abraham | One can also be dirty on Wednesdays. |

*Yenta opens a drawer and takes out underwear. She hands it to Shloimele, but he doesn't take it.*

| | |
|---|---|
| Shloimele | Be so good, put it down. |
| Abraham | He doesn't take anything from the hand of a woman. |
| Yenta | *Puts it down.* He's the only one who seems to notice that I'm a woman. |
| Shloimele | We are all created by God. *Exits.* |
| Yenta | If the master has something to do here, I will come back later. |
| Abraham | You can clean up. Where's Zirel? |
| Yenta | She lies down and sleeps in the middle of the day. She doesn't sleep a wink all night, and then falls off her feet all morning. |

| | |
|---|---|
| Abraham | How do you know she doesn't sleep at night? She told you? |
| Yenta | I hear. |
| Abraham | You don't sleep either? |
| Yenta | No one sleeps in this house, not even the master. |
| Abraham | I sleep. |
| Yenta | I hear everything. When the master sighs, my heart aches. |
| Abraham | I wasn't aware that I sigh. |
| Yenta | How long should a man mourn? One is not allowed to grieve for the dead forever. |
| Abraham | I know, Yenta, but what can I do when there's sadness inside? I think about her day and night. |
| Yenta | Don't I do the same thing? The mistress stands before my eyes as though she were alive. The moment I close my eyes, I hear her voice. |
| Abraham | If you, a stranger, cannot forger her, what can I do? |
| Yenta | What the earth covers has to be forgotten. |
| Abraham | If you can, you forget. |
| Yenta | Sometimes I wish I would never have fallen into this house. |
| Abraham | You don't have to stay here. Go and find a husband. |
| Yenta | What husband? When you are accustomed to silk, you can no longer wear sackcloth. |

| | |
|---|---|
| Abraham | This is my misfortune, but you are younger than I— |
| Yenta | How much younger? I lie on my bed and toss around as if with fever. A fire burns my insides. I keep drinking water all night long. |
| Abraham | You too? |
| Yenta | And when I fall asleep, the real Gehenna begins. |
| Abraham | I understand you too well. I'll go downstairs and let you clean up here. *He exits.* |
| Yenta | A curse, a curse. This house is like quicksand. Step in with one foot, and you begin to sink. Where shall I go? To whom? A *stranger* he calls me! I wish I *were* a stranger. Oy, mother, there's turmoil inside me. *She sees the storybook, opens it in the middle, and begins to read aloud.* "And when the queen realized that the king stopped thinking about her, she went to the witch Cunegunde and said to her: Cunegunde, help me turn the king's heart to love me again, and to yearn for my lap, day and night. And Cunegunde said to her: My queen, when the king falls asleep, enter his room with three of your maids, encircle his bed seven times. Cut off one of your braids and wrap it around his neck. Take water in which you have washed your breasts |

and sprinkle it on his forehead. Then
gaze into the mirror and there you will
see the one who robbed you of your
love. Spit at her and stick your tongue
out to her. Gnash your teeth and wave
your fists at her and recite:

> Machlat, Nahama's daughter
> Begone, disappear.
> The north wind should strike
> Your face and your rear.
>
> Daughter of Satan,
> My house avoid;
> Your bosom be dry,
> Your womb a void.
>
> Green in the eyes,
> Pox on your tongue.
> Blood and poison
> In your devil's dung.
>
> Extinguished should be
> Your fire in the sea;
> Black death entrap
> Your sinful lap.
>
> Return, oh king
> With renewed lust
> To my loins
> And to my breast."

What a book! I could read it day and night. *Begins to sweep the floor and dust the furniture. Listens for a while.* She's asleep, asleep. *Opens the commode and takes out Zirel's wedding gown and veil, and puts them on. Looks into mirror.* Not an ugly bride. He would certainly not poison himself with me. A stranger he calls me. Here is my bridegroom. *Imaginary Abraham enters.* Come, my beloved, don't be shy. Lead me under the canopy. Play musicians, drum drummer. Blind Shimele, let's hear the trumpet. Zeinvele, sound the clarinet. Let there be joy.

> The Angels are gay,
> In Heaven sits the King
> Playing with the Wild Ox
> And with Leviathan,
> Blessing bride and bridegroom.

*Yenta begins to dance with the broom.* Now jester, let's hear your voice.

*Jester enters.*

Jester       Bride, bride, cry, cry
I'll bring you a goblet of wine.
Bride, bride, laugh, laugh
Marrying your beloved is fine.

Happy bride, cut off your hair,
Your luck should really shine,
Grace be yours, like the sun is clear,
Take ablutions at the right time.

Abraham    According to the book, a man's first
wife is destined to him, but he gets a
second because of his merits. I must
have done great deeds to deserve a gem
like Yenta. Only God knows how sweet
she is and how devoted to me. Come,
my bride, this is my happiest day. I will
never leave town, even for business, but
stay with you, talk to you, listen to your
advice. I will not follow Shloimele's
example, but kiss you, caress you, and
in the evening we will read the storybook together and tell each other
wonderful tales—and at night—

*Bride and bridegroom dance holding a kerchief between
them.*

Jester    Enough dancing. Come good groom,
We'll lead you to a darkened room,
A sweet secret will be revealed,
Since secrets are to be unveiled.

*Abraham and Jester leave. Yenta gazes into the mirror and
falls in a faint. Real Abraham enters.*

| | |
|---|---|
| Abraham | What happened? She fainted! I heard your fall. *He rubs her temples.* Get up, get up! |
| Yenta | *Awakening.* Oy! |
| Abraham1 | Why did you put Zirel's wedding gown on? What made you faint? |
| Yenta | Master, please, let me be. |
| Abraham | Have you, God forbid, lost your mind? |
| Yenta | If you don't have your own, you put on someone else's. |
| Abraham | God willing, you will have your own wedding gown, and bridegroom to boot. *Raises her and seats her in a chair.* |
| Yenta | When? I'm tired of waiting. |
| Abraham | He who is destined for you will not be stolen by anyone else. |
| Yenta | They steal everything. The world is made of thieves and swindlers. |
| Abraham | Take the wedding gown off. If Zirel sees this, it will cause her grief. |
| Yenta | The hooks are so tight that I can't unhook myself. |
| Abraham | Stand still and I'll help you. *Tries to unhook her.* |
| Yenta | Is it opening? |
| Abraham | Who fastened this for you? |
| Yenta | Things happen by themselves. |
| Abraham | Wait. *He pulls the dress and it falls off. She stands in her undergarments.* Oy, the evil spirit. *He runs away.* |

Yenta    Pious but sweet. If he were mine, I would dance and praise God ten times a day. *Lifts her broom.* Meanwhile you are my husband. *Kisses it and dances with it.*

*Curtain*

# SCENE 4

*R*eb Yoyets, the Jew of Babylon—tall, lean, with a white beard, wearing a fez on his head, with a black and red striped robe and sandals—speaks to Shloimele and Zirel.

| | |
|---|---|
| Reb Yoyets | *To Zirel.* Perhaps you have a knot in your dress? |
| Zirel | There are no knots in the dress I'm wearing. |
| Reb Yoyets | Let me see. Perhaps an elflock in your hair? Take off your headcovering. |
| Shloimele | It's forbidden. A woman should never take off her headcovering. A woman's hair incites a man to sinful thoughts. |
| Reb Yoyets | Everything is kosher to effect a cure. When a woman gives birth, one is even allowed to desecrate Shabbat. |
| Zirel | *Removes bonnet.* See, Reb Yoyetz, no elflocks. |
| Shloimele | You have long hair! Have you stopped shaving your head? |

| Reb Yoyets | You, her husband, don't know she lets her hair grow? |
| Zirel | What does he know? |
| Reb Yoyets | You have no elflocks either. |
| Shloimele | If you don't shave your head tonight— |
| Zirel | What are you going to do? |
| Shloimele | Your kind prolongs the exile. |
| Reb Yoyets | *To Shloimele.* Since she has no knots or elflocks, I'm going to examine you. |
| Shloimele | Don't touch me! These examinations are defiling. |
| Zirel | It is better to be defiled than dead. |

*Shloimele removes his gabardine, remains in his fringed garment.*

| Reb Yoyets | *Searches inside Shloimele's clothes.* I don't see any knots. Remove your skullcap. |
| Shloimele | *Holds skullcap fast.* God forbid! |
| Reb Yoyets | You never knows where the witchcraft is hidden. Sometimes even in a sidelock. |
| Shloimele | You're not allowed to stand with a bare head. |
| Zirel | Imagine that you're in the mikveh. *She tears off his skullcap.* |
| Reb Yoyets | You have no elflocks either, so how come you two can't get together? |
| Shloimele | We do get together, but— |
| Reb Yoyets | Something is not in order here. *Walks around and sniffs the walls.* |

*Abraham enters.*

| | |
|---|---|
| Abraham | Well, children, how are things going? |
| Shloimele | I have to leave. |
| Abraham | *He holds him fast by the shoulder.* No, you'll stay unless you wish to be rid of my daughter. |
| Shloimele | Reb Abraham, people like him destroy the world. *Points at Jew of Babylon.* |
| Zirel | I wish he *would* destroy it. |
| Shloimele | Do you hear, Reb Abraham, how she blasphemes? |
| Reb Yoyets | The world is not such a bargain. Even our sages have said, "It would have been better for humankind not to have been created." It is written about the Almighty that he regretted creating humans. |
| Shloimele | Every word in the Torah is studded with mysteries. May I put on my gabardine now? |
| Reb Yoyets | Not yet. Take off your fringed garment. There may be witchcraft hidden there. |
| Shloimele | In the fringed garment? Never! |
| Zirel | He doesn't even take it off at night. |
| Abraham | Even the holy rabbis don't wear their fringes at night. |
| Zirel | Sometimes I'm astonished that he doesn't come to me in his prayer shawl and phylacteries. |

| | |
|---|---|
| Shloimele | Sacrilege. Please, let me go. |
| Abraham | Stay, Shloimele, we're trying to help you. |
| Reb Yoyets | Is the plate with the incense pan ready? |
| Abraham | Everything's ready. *Calls out.* Yenta! Bring plate with the incense pan. |

*Yenta enters with an incense pan full of live coals on a flat silver dish.*

| | |
|---|---|
| Reb Yoyets | *Puts incense on the coals. Removes a piece of wax from an inside pocket and holds it over the coals.* |
| Shloimele | Reb Abraham, this is idolatry. |
| Abraham | Didn't Aaron carry a firepan and incense into the Tabernacle? |
| Reb Yoyets | *Pours wax over plate and makes certain designs.* So I see. Hm. Hm. Hm. *Rubs his forehead with his left hand.* What do you see, Zirel? Look into the plate. |
| Zirel | Something like the image of a person. |
| Reb Yoyets | Male or female? |
| Zirel | Male. |
| Reb Yoyets | And what do you see, Shloimele? |
| Shloimele | I refuse to look. |
| Abraham | Look! We want to help you. |
| Shloimele | These are the doings of warlocks. It is prohibited by the Law of Moses. I'd rather be divorced than lose the world to come. |

| | |
|---|---|
| Abraham | I take the sin upon me. I will take all your lashings in Gehenna. |
| Reb Yoyets | *To Shloimele.* Please, look and tell me what you see. |
| Shloimele | *He stares.* I don't know what I see. It's something strange. |
| Reb Yoyets | What is it? A man? An animal? |
| Shloimele | Neither. |
| Zirel | A vegetable? |
| Yenta | *Laughs nervously.* |
| Abraham | Yenta, be quiet. |
| Reb Yoyets | I ask you again, what is it you see? |
| Shloimele | Perhaps a person. |
| Reb Yoyets | Male of female? |
| Shloimele | *Again stares for a while.* Perhaps male. |
| Reb Yoyets | You too? Strange events are already revealed but there's more to come. *He lifts the incense pan and walks around murmuring. Then he returns to the table.* Do you have a birthmark on your body? |
| Zirel | A birthmark? What could that mean? |
| Reb Yoyets | Some people are born with a little mouse on the skin, or a speck of honey on the breast, and although one does not realize it, they wreak havoc in a person's life. |
| Abraham | As far as I know, my daughter has no blemish. |
| Zirel | I have no mice and no specks on my body. |
| Reb Yoyets | How about Shloimele? |

| | |
|---|---|
| Shloimele | I don't know what he's talking about. |
| Abraham | I've been to the mikveh with him and I haven't seen anything unusual. |
| Reb Yoyets | Some unclean entity has settled in this house, but what it is I still don't know. I will hang talismans on the walls. *Hangs talismans on the walls, murmuring and gesticulating.* For the time being, it may help. |
| Shloimele | Am I allowed to go now? |
| Zirel | What's your hurry? The Messiah hasn't come yet. |
| Shloimele | He may any minute. |
| Zirel | Since he's been imagining he's bringing the Messiah, he's been sleeping in his breeches and stockings. |
| Shloimele | *Reproachfully.* I asked you to keep it a secret. |
| Zirel | How many secrets can I keep? He's fasting and it's a secret. He lines his shoes with pebbles and it's a secret again. Why hasn't he come yet? Because you urinated in the snow? *Laughs.* |
| Yenta | Now I understand. I wanted to wash the young master's breeches, but they were nowhere to be found. |
| Abraham | What is the sense of sleeping in one's breeches and stockings? |
| Shloimele | When the Messiah arrives, I should be ready to meet him. |

| | |
|---|---|
| Yenta | How long does it take to put these things on? |
| Reb Yoyets | Forgive me, young man, but this is ignorance. Everyone knows that the Messiah won't come at night, only in the daytime. |
| Shloimele | It's not written anywhere that he must come only in the daytime. All I know is that he won't come on Shabbos or holidays. |
| Reb Yoyets | I clearly remember reading that the Messiah won't come at night. |
| Shloimele | In what book? They invent things. All they want is to delay the redemption. They are afraid that, when the Messiah comes, their abominations will be revealed. |
| Reb Yoyets | I came here to help you, and you're insulting me. Why? |
| Shloimele | Jews don't live by the signs of constellations and witchcraft. We don't need anyone to act as an intermediary to God. When Jews are in need, they can pray directly to their Lord in Heaven. |
| Reb Yoyets | Even this isn't true. There are devils, goblins, mockers, destroyers, imps, sprites, and every one of these creatures has its own powers. I should know. I've waged war on them all my life. As I talk to you, young man, they surround me |

|             |                                                                                                 |
| ----------- | ----------------------------------------------------------------------------------------------- |
|             | and try to destroy me. I have to use all my resources to prevent it.                             |
| Yenta       | Oy, Mama! Oy, Mama! *Shudders.*                                                                  |
| Shloimele   | If one serves God, the evil host is powerless.                                                   |
| Reb Yoyets  | Since you are a scholar, you should know that each man has ten thousand devils on his right side, and a thousand on his left. And how about the dead? |
| Yenta       | What is it with the dead?                                                                        |
| Reb Yoyets  | They're not dead. Everything that has ever lived continues to live. They are all here. Adam, Noah, the generation that built the Tower of Babel, the generation of the Flood. Sometimes, when I sit at my window and look out, I see the armies of the Pharaohs, Nebuchadnezzar. They march equipped with swords, spears, and suits of armor. |
| Yenta       | What do they march toward?                                                                       |
| Reb Yoyets  | They march. Others ride horses.                                                                  |
| Abraham     | Dead horses?                                                                                     |
| Reb Yoyets  | There is no death.                                                                               |
| Zirel       | Is my mother still here?                                                                         |
| Reb Yoyets  | Whatever was is still here.                                                                      |
| Zirel       | Where is she?                                                                                    |
| Shloimele   | In Paradise.                                                                                     |
| Reb Yoyets  | Sometimes in Paradise, and sometimes somewhere else. They don't remain in                       |

one place. There is constant wandering. It is said that every saint possesses 310 worlds, and from one world to the next is a distance of 500 years.

Yenta — I'm afraid.

Zirel — Why doesn't mother show herself to me? I would give half of my years to have one look at her.

Reb Yoyets — You don't see her, but she watches you.

Yenta — Sometimes at night, when I go to drink water from the pitcher, I feel her presence.

Shloimele — "The mysteries belong to God, our God." We should serve the Almighty, not delve into what is hidden from us.

Reb Yoyets — As I said, I have to return to Lublin, but I'll come back.

Abraham — When, Reb Yoyetz?

Reb Yoyets — As soon as possible. As to you, young man, stop sleeping in your breeches. You will not bring the Redemption that way.

Shloimele — The redeemer will soon arrive. These are the birth throes of his coming. May I go already?

Reb Yoyets — Wait! Before I leave, I want to look at the mezuzah.

Yenta — Shall I take it off? *Removes the mezuzah, gives it to the Jew of Babylon. He unwraps it and reads it.*

47

| | |
|---|---|
| Reb Yoyets | "Shema Israel, the Lord our God, the Lord is One, and—" *Suddenly.* The letter aleph has faded! |
| All of them | Faded?! |
| Abraham | I'll send for Moshe the scribe to have it fixed. If not, we are all in danger. |
| Shloimele | Now I understand everything. |
| Reb Yoyets | You don't understand everything. Of course, the mezuzah should be corrected, but there are powers which even the mezuzah cannot curb. |
| Shloimele | One is not allowed to be without a proper mezuzah for a single moment. |
| Reb Yoyets | You can go now, but don't be a fool. The Talmud says that three things enliven the spirit of a man: a beautiful house, a beautiful wife, and beautiful possessions. You have all three of them, but— |
| Zirel | An old man, and he speaks like a young one. |
| Reb Yoyets | Believe me, daughter, one never gets old. |
| Shloimele | I'm going. *Exits.* |
| Abraham | What shall I do with him? A saintly man, but not of this world. |
| Reb Yoyets | I'm afraid that you won't bake any bread from this dough. |
| Zirel | Do you hear, father? |
| Abraham | He had holy ancestors. I don't dare defy them. |

| | |
|---|---|
| Reb Yoyets | Ancestors don't interfere in such matters. If they did, none of us could exist. |
| Zirel | Father, if I can't get a divorce, I'll kill myself. |
| Reb Yoyets | Don't lose hope, Zirel. I'm going away, but I will return. Just wait for me. |
| Yenta | Master, may I ask the miracle worker something? |
| Abraham | What do you want to ask? |
| Yenta | Does the master remember how I fainted? |
| Abraham | Surely I remember. It happened only recently. |
| Yenta | I saw something in the mirror. |
| Zirel | In the mirror? |
| Reb Yoyets | What did you see? |
| Yenta | What I saw passed so quickly that I couldn't be certain. Like the quickest bird. |
| Reb Yoyets | What was it, a man, an animal, a rodent? |
| Yenta | Something like an ape. |
| Abraham | And that made you faint? |
| Yenta | Yes, master. *Bursts out crying* |
| Reb Yoyets | I will sit in my wagon all night, and since I don't sleep, I will try to think this through. |
| Zirel | Why don't you sleep, Reb Yoyetz? |
| Reb Yoyets | They don't let me. |
| Zirel | Who? The demons? |

Reb Yoyets    Who else? What I go through, only
              God knows, and sometimes I think
              that even he doesn't know everything.

          *Curtain*

# SCENE 4

*A knocking. Yenta and Zirel both come into the room.*

Yenta     *In a frightened voice.* The mistress hears?

Zirel      Knocks, knocks. Why do they bang so loudly?

Yenta     As if stones were falling.

Zirel      Like a house being wrecked.

Yenta     Someone's walking around all night long. I keep hearing heavy footsteps.

Zirel      Where do you hear them, in the hallway?

Yenta     Sometimes in the hallway, sometimes on the stairs.

Zirel      Yesterday they dragged something across the attic. I thought they moved the closet or the old wooden trunk. I lit a candle and went to look, but everything was in its place.

*Sounds of glass breaking.*

Yenta     *Terrified.* Did the mistress just hear that?

Zirel      I'm not deaf.

| Yenta | It sounded like the smashing of a glass by a bridegroom under the canopy. |
|---|---|
| Zirel | Or of a drunk in a tavern. |
| Yenta | Perhaps they're having a wedding. |
| Zirel | Who—with whom? |
| Yenta | They also have males and females. There are even Jewish demons and Christian demons. |
| Zirel | I wonder what mine is. |
| Yenta | What do you mean? |
| Zirel | I'm only joking. And how do you recognize a Jew? Is he circumcised? |
| Yenta | Oh, how the mistress talks! |
| Zirel | The only way to sin in Krashnik. |

*A crash is heard.*

| Zirel | The house is collapsing. |
|---|---|
| Yenta | A disaster is coming! |
| Zirel | I have to put up with it, but why should you suffer? All roads are open to you. |
| Yenta | Nothing is open. When I was hired here as a child, for the first time I tasted life. Your sweet mother, your kind father, well, and you yourself— |

*A vase falls from a shelf.*

| Zirel | Mazel Tov! |
|---|---|
| Yenta | They're breaking dishes too. |
| Zirel | They may break our heads next. |

Yenta   Mistress, what's happened to us? *Falls on Zirel's neck and cries.* Come, mistress, let's see what's happening in the kitchen.

Zirel   Go yourself, Yenta, I'll stay here.

Yenta   Are you not afraid to stay alone with them?

Zirel   Even this is better than the drudgery of my life.

Yenta   Terrible! *Exits.*

Zirel   *Long pause.* Well, let's hear what you can do. *A knock is heard.* Another one! *Another knock is heard.* Now two, one after the other! *Two knocks.* In that case, maybe we can have a conversation. One knock will signify yes, and two knocks no. Do you agree? *One knock.* Will my husband divorce me? *Two knocks.* Will we be together? *Two knocks.* Not divorced and not together? Will I be a widow? *Two knocks.* Will he become a widower? *Two knocks.* He won't divorce me and we won't be together. I won't be a widow and he won't be a widower. How is this possible? Will he leave me a deserted wife? *Two knocks.* Even demons must have some sense. Will my father move away from Krashnik? *Two knocks.* Will Yenta leave us? *Two knocks.* Will I get sick? *Two knocks.* Will I be healthy? *Two knocks.* Well, I better not ask anymore.

Yenta   *Enters.* The Jew of Babylon is here.

Zirel   Tell him to come in while I get dressed.

| Yenta | You want to hear something strange? The saltshaker suddenly lifted itself off the shelf and sailed towards the oven. There it turned upside down and all the salt spilled into a pot of soup. Then it fell to the floor and broke into shards. |
| Zirel | Did you see this yourself? |
| Yenta | I should live so to see my destined one with me under the canopy. |
| Zirel | I used to think that demons were clever, now I see that they can be very silly. |
| Yenta | These are mockers, not demons. |
| Zirel | I'm going to change. *Exits.* |
| Yenta | If all these things don't kill me, it means I'm stronger than iron. *Exits.* |

*For a while the stage is empty, then the Jew of Babylon enters with Yenta. He carries a bag that he puts on the table.*

| Reb Yoyets | She isn't here? |
| Yenta | She went to change, to make herself beautiful for you. |
| Reb Yoyets | Well, so it is … |
| Yenta | Holy miracle worker, you will never know what we've been through. We haven't sleep nights. The master of the house has completely neglected his business. The younger master has refused to sleep at home. He sleeps in the study house. |

| | |
|---|---|
| Reb Yoyets | He's looking for any chance he can get to stay away from his beautiful wife. |
| Yenta | It's the truth. Other men would consider themselves lucky to have such a wife. |
| Reb Yoyets | Give an ox the best cutlet, and he won't eat it. He needs straw. |
| Yenta | Oy, how well said. Holy miracle worker, I want to ask you something |
| Reb Yoyets | What's that? |
| Yenta | What I want to ask makes me ashamed. |
| Reb Yoyets | Those who want something strongly set aside all shame. |
| Yenta | I was told that—I've heard that— |
| Reb Yoyets | Speak clearly. |
| Yenta | I read in the storybook that there's some charm that evokes— |
| Reb Yoyets | Love? |
| Yenta | How did you guess? |
| Reb Yoyets | Who is he? Someone from the village? |
| Yenta | Yes, someone from Krashnik. |
| Reb Yoyets | A bachelor, a divorced man, a widower? |
| Yenta | A widower. |
| Reb Yoyets | Did you declare your love to him and he turned you down? |
| Yenta | I was too shy to do that. |
| Reb Yoyets | Perhaps he's also shy. |
| Yenta | He's a highly respected citizen and I'm only a servant. |
| Reb Yoyets | Respected people have the same desires as rascals and lechers. Abraham, our |

patriarch, married our grandmother Sarah and then took Hagar as a concubine. When Sarah died, he took Keturah, and she bore him Zimran, Jokshan, Medan, Midian, Ishbak, and Shuah.

Yenta   My beloved only thinks of his dead wife.

Reb Yoyets   The dead live, but they cannot darn your stockings.

Yenta   I do everything for him. *Is frightened and covers her mouth.* What did I say? I'm also an ox and I should eat straw too.

Reb Yoyets   You kiss me and everything will be as you wish.

Yenta   Oy, what are you saying? You make fun of me. *Giggles.*

Reb Yoyets   It's the right cure. All the young women who've kissed me have gotten good husbands.

Yenta   It's forbidden. This is a sin.

Reb Yoyets   I take the sin upon me.

Yenta   In the morality book, it is written that for such transgressions one lies on a bed of nails.

Reb Yoyets   I'm going to lie on it for years, so I'll lie a few days longer.

Yenta   What do you need my kisses for? You're an old man.

Reb Yoyets   The old need them more than the young.

| | |
|---|---|
| Yenta | Someone may see us. |
| Reb Yoyets | While you've hesitated, you could have given me a dozen kisses. |
| Yenta | Will this really make my master love me? |
| Reb Yoyets | Yes, but make it long and passionate. |
| Yenta | Mother of mine, the things that happen to me! *Kisses him as he embraces her.* Enough. |
| Reb Yoyets | Once more! |
| Yenta | *Kisses him again.* He kisses like a young man, not like an old one. *Kisses him again of her own free will.* |
| Zirel | *Enters.* What do I see? |
| Yenta | Mistress! *Runs out crying.* |
| Zirel | *To Reb Yoyets.* At your age! |
| Reb Yoyets | The poet has said: "Old men die young." If your husband is really a kabbalist, he must have told you that the whole universe is based on copulation. God copulates with the Shekhinah. Jacob continues to copulate with Rachel, Leah, Billah, Zilphah. Even among the rocks, there are males and females. Put away two stones, one a male and the other a female, and they will slowly approach, and the male stone will mount the female stone. |
| Zirel | He never told me such things. |
| Reb Yoyets | How beautiful you are. Looking at you makes my thighs quiver. |

*A knocking is heard.*

| | |
|---|---|
| Zirel | Meanwhile, they're tearing the house apart. |
| Reb Yoyets | To you this is new. These things have been torturing me since childhood. My father was a pious man. He sent me to *heder* like all the other boys, but the spirits were already after me. At night they knotted my sidelocks. I lay awake in bed and in the darkness they danced and braided their hair around my neck. They licked me and whispered secrets into my ear. |
| Zirel | Didn't you tell your parents? |
| Reb Yoyets | I already knew these afflictions cannot be told. |
| Zirel | What did they want from you? |
| Reb Yoyets | The same as from you: love. |
| Zirel | From a little boy? |
| Reb Yoyets | The soul is never little. |
| Zirel | How come they leave others in peace? |
| Reb Yoyets | They make their choices. |
| Zirel | Are you really from Babylon? |
| Reb Yoyets | No, I was born in Lublin, but at the age of fourteen I had to leave home. I left in order to find relief from them and wandered a long time, until I reached Babylon, Egypt, Yemen, and Persia. |
| Zirel | Do they still desire you? |

| | |
|---|---|
| Reb Yoyets | They tear pieces out of me. Though I cure others, I am sicker than all of them. Last night I didn't sleep a wink in the wagon. They danced in front of the horses. They screeched and whistled and made the horses rear. The coachman was so frightened, he tried to leave the wagon and run off on foot. |
| Zirel | Did you ever love these females? |
| Reb Yoyets | I made love to all of them and this was my undoing. |
| Zirel | Are they better than human females? |
| Reb Yoyets | Better and more abandoned. But once you begin with them, there's no end to your troubles. While you are lying with one, another tries to get you to lie with her. Shame is something they don't know. |
| Zirel | And with all this you still kiss Yenta? |
| Reb Yoyets | One can only escape from them to the daughters of Eve. |
| Zirel | Did you have many human wives? |
| Reb Yoyets | More than I have hair in my beard. |
| Zirel | What happened to them? |
| Reb Yoyets | I left them all. |
| Zirel | Not one of them suited you? |
| Reb Yoyets | No … But I never lost hope of finding the right one. |
| Zirel | Is this why you fondled our maid? |
| Reb Yoyets | This is why I yearn for you. |
| Zirel | Another man's wife? |

| | |
|---|---|
| Reb Yoyets | If he's not a man, you're not his wife. |
| Zirel | What would you do if I said yes? |
| Reb Yoyets | I would kiss your lips. Then I would give you this gift. *Takes a string of pearls out of his bag.* |
| Zirel | What magnificent pearls! |
| Reb Yoyets | I've never lacked for gold or gems. |
| Zirel | Are you an alchemist? |
| Reb Yoyets | I don't need to indulge in alchemy. I've cured the rich and they shower me with treasures. I've made the mute talk, the deaf hear. I help epileptics and those who've suffered from jaundice and leprosy. I've made the insane sane, and I returned potency to the impotent. I've cured everyone except myself. |
| Zirel | Why are you trembling? Are you cold? |
| Reb Yoyets | I'm trembling. But I'm not cold. |
| Zirel | Where would you take me if I were willing to become what you propose? |
| Reb Yoyets | To India, China, Africa. I've discovered an island that the evil ones don't know about. |
| Zirel | Really! You arouse my curiosity. |
| Reb Yoyets | I saw all your powers the moment I laid my eye on you. |
| Zirel | Only one eye? |
| Reb Yoyets | My right eye is almost blind, but my left sees too much. |
| Zirel | What did you see in me? |
| Reb Yoyets | A fire that will never be extinguished. |

| | |
|---|---|
| Zirel | This fire might burn you. |
| Reb Yoyets | Not to ashes. |
| Zirel | What can I do, Reb Yoyetz? My spouse refuses to divorce me. The house is being torn apart. My father is all alone. Every night is a nightmare. |
| Reb Yoyets | Be mine and I'll pull you out of your swamp. Through all my sufferings, I've learned of pleasures that no other human has ever tasted. |

*There's a strong pounding, pouring water, the howl of a beast.*

| | |
|---|---|
| Zirel | I'm afraid of this night. I have a premonition it's going to be my last one. |
| Reb Yoyets | Sit down and I'll begin my exorcism. |
| Zirel | Yes, do something! |

*Zirel sits down and turns the pages of the storybook. Reb Yoyets opens his bag and takes out a ram's horn and a jar of ashes. He tries to blow the horn, but only short sounds come out.*

| | |
|---|---|
| Zirel | The people of Krashnik are going to think it's Rosh Hashanah. |
| Reb Yoyets | For me, it's always a Day of Judgment. |
| Zirel | What kinds of ashes are these? |
| Reb Yoyets | From a black cat whose mother was also a black cat. First born and the daughter of a first born. |
| Zirel | Did you burn her? |

| | |
|---|---|
| Reb Yoyets | If one must, one must. *Removes a palm branch from the bag, pours ashes over it, goes over to the walls and shakes it.* In the name of the Holy Angel Metatron, in the name of Sandalphon the Lord, in the name of Katriel, Lumiel, Malkiel, Emiel, I beseech you to leave this place and go back to your wastelands. If not, the curses that were evoked on Mount Ebal will fall on your hairless heads. Shadai—destroy Satan. *Kuzu, b'muchzas, Kuzu—* |

*A crash—as if the roof has fallen in.*

| | |
|---|---|
| Zirel | They're not afraid of your Angels. |
| Reb Yoyets | I haven't finished yet. *Tries to approach the mirror. Stops, startled. The palm branch falls down and the Jew of Babylon begins to wrangle and wrestle as if attacked by an unseen entity. He groans and brings out rattling sounds as if being choked.* |
| Zirel | *Jumps in alarm.* My God, Reb Yoyetz! |
| Reb Yoyets | *With a choked voice.* Zirel, help me. *He falls on floor and continues to wrestle desperately with an unseen one.* |
| Zirel | *Screams.* Father! Yenta! *Abraham and Yenta come running.* |
| Abraham | What's happening? |
| Yenta | Master! Oh, my God. *She embraces Abraham in fear.* |

Zirel            *In panic.* Lift him up! Help him!

*All three try to raise him but don't succeed. He continues grappling and convulsing.*

Yenta           *Gevalt!* Help, help.
Shloimele       *Rushes in, frightened.* Shema Israel, the
                Lord our God, the Lord is one. *Dashes
                out in fear.*
Yenta           Master, master! *Clutches and kisses him.*
Abraham         Have you lost your mind?

*In desperation, Zirel raises the palm branch, waves it over Jew of Babylon and pours ashes over him. His struggle slowly stops. He groans deeply and raises himself.*

Reb Yoyets      *To Zirel.* You've saved my life.
Zirel           What was it?
Reb Yoyets      He had the strength and stench of a
                monkey. I was never assailed in such a
                wild way.
Yenta           He's as pale as death.
Zirel           It's Hurmizah. *To Yenta.* Take him to
                his room. Make his bed. Call the
                leecher.
Reb Yoyets      No leecher can help me, but I will have
                to lie down.
Abraham         Was he a demon?
Reb Yoyets      I could not see him, but he stunk like
                an ape.
Yenta           *Cries,* Mother, what's happening to us?

| | |
|---|---|
| Reb Yoyets | *To Yenta.* I'll be fine. But keep watch over Zirel. She's not to be left alone one moment during this night. |
| Abraham | What do they want, Reb Yoyetz? |
| Reb Yoyets | They want Zirel, but they won't get her. |
| Abraham | Come, Reb Yoyetz. |

*They leave, with Abraham helping Reb Yoyetz and supporting him.*

| | |
|---|---|
| Yenta | I hope he doesn't die tonight. |
| Zirel | He won't last long. *She lies down on the divan, tries to read from the storybook, but seems to be having difficulty seeing. Rubs her eyes and says to Yenta:* You read to me. |
| Yenta | What shall I read? |
| Zirel | About love. *Long pause.* I'm in love, too. |
| Yenta | In love? With whom? |
| Zirel | With a devil. |
| Yenta | Oh, you're joking. |
| Zirel | No, I'm serious. |
| Yenta | What do you mean? Have you seen him? |
| Zirel | Yes, I saw him. He declared his love to me. |
| Yenta | Where? How? |
| Zirel | In the mirror. *Points to it.* |
| Yenta | I don't believe you. But you frighten me just the same. What does he look like? |
| Zirel | A monkey. |
| Yenta | That's what I thought I saw. |

| | |
|---|---|
| Zirel | He wanted to talk to me, not you. When he saw you, he vanished. |
| Yenta | You love a devil? |
| Zirel | I'm tired of men. They're either pious, old, or frail. My devil is ugly but strong, evil and passionate. He really wants me and if he appears again, he may get me. |
| Yenta | I know that you don't mean what you say, but don't say such things. These words are dangerous. "Don't open your mouth to Satan." |
| Zirel | There are no real men in Krashnik. Only boys with long beards. Sometimes I suspect that there are no real men anywhere. The whole world is one big Krashnik. |
| Yenta | Isn't your father a man? |
| Zirel | He's not Lot and he doesn't drink wine. |
| Yenta | Oh, mistress, I'm in love too. I love you and your father. I would give my life for either of you. |
| Zirel | I need Hurmizah, not your life. But he may never appear again. I scolded him. He's very proud. |
| Yenta | Aren't you afraid of God's punishment? |
| Zirel | My misery is so great that I can't imagine anything worse. |
| Yenta | What pains you so, mistress? |
| Zirel | Of all the pains, boredom is worst. I open my eyes in the morning and I |

|       |                                                                                         |
|-------|-----------------------------------------------------------------------------------------|
|       | wish it were night. At night I lie awake and can hardly wait for daybreak. I've read this book a thousand times already. When Shloimele comes to me, I have to try hard not to vomit. Yenta, Gehenna is closer than you imagine. |
| Yenta | What do you mean? |
| Zirel | Krashnik *is* Gehenna! |
| Yenta | Perhaps the Jew of Babylon can help you. |
| Zirel | He suffers from the same sickness. You saw how helpless he was when my sweet devil attacked him. |
| Yenta | God will forgive you, mistress. It is not you speaking, but your tortured soul. |
| Zirel | Read to me, Yenta, perhaps it will help me fall asleep. |

# SCENE 5

| | |
|---|---|
| Yenta | *Reads to Zirel.* The island of Crete was ruled by a king named Malkitzedek. He has a daughter whose name was Buddadah, and she was always alone. She ate alone, she slept alone, and alone she read her storybooks. The truth is that Malkitzedek was a wicked man who wanted his daughter for himself and was jealous not only of men but also of women having anything to do with her. She was served by a eunuch called Maruch Ashach, who was mute because the king had his tongue cut out to prevent him from telling court secrets. One day, the princess Buddadah heard a voice calling: Buddadah, I yearn for you, and I know that you yearn for me. How long can we go on pining away for each other? Go into the garden at night and you will see four cats, two white and two black. These will be my messengers. They |

|       | will surround you and dance around you. Then they will lead you into my palace... *Yenta yawns.* I can't read anymore, my eyes are closing. I need a rest. *Stops reading, dozes off.* |
|-------|---|
| Zirel | Why don't you continue? Oh, she fell asleep. *Zirel gets up and walks around the room. Approaches the mirror. To herself:* I miss him constantly. I have nothing to lose anyway. *Raises her voice.* Hurmizah, son of Onan, I made a mistake by driving you away. I don't need their spells and incantations. I want only you, Hurmizah. This is the truth. *The mirror is empty.* Playing hard to get? *In a sing song:* Come, my devil. I am ready for you. The fires of all my nights are burning in my lap. A thirst no man can quench consumes my insides. I constantly see your yellow eyes, Your animal fur, your long arms, your evil tongue. Bite me like a snake. Pierce me like a bull. What God has rejected, Satan must take. |

*Hurmizah appears in the mirror.*

| Zirel | Hurmizah! |
|-------|---|
| Demon | I had swore by Asmodeus's beard that you would never see my face again. But |

|        | I heard your voice and I'm aware of your yearning. |
|--------|----------------------------------------------------|
| Zirel  | Hurmizah, my beloved. Take me to Lublin, to Krakow, to wherever you are. |
| Demon  | I'm neither in Lublin nor in Krakow. |
| Zirel  | Where are you? |
| Demon  | In Sodom. |
| Zirel  | In Sodom? |
| Demon  | I'm not called Hurmizah any more, but Lord Hurmizah. I'm one of the rulers of the House of Esau. I live in Asmodeus's castle. |
| Zirel  | How big you are! How beautiful in your ugliness. Larger horns, longer tail. How did you grow way? |
| Demon  | Not by reciting Psalms. |
| Zirel  | I tried to deny it, but I craved for you incessantly. |
| Demon  | Once a female has crossed my path, she can never forget me. |
| Zirel  | What do you do? How do you live? You're surely married already. |
| Demon  | Marriage in Sodom? One look and consent is given. |
| Zirel  | What do you bid me to do, Hurmizah? |
| Demon  | Come with me. |
| Zirel  | *Hesitating.* Since you have all these she-devils, what do you need me for? |
| Demon  | My father was a human and the desire for human flesh is still with me. |

| | |
|---|---|
| Zirel | What have I got that they don't have? |
| Demon | A lot of fear, a little shame. The daughter of Eve covers and uncovers. They are always uncovered. |
| Zirel | What are we going to do in Sodom? |
| Demon | You will sit on my lap and plait tresses in my beard. We'll eat almonds and drink mead. Evenings you will dance for my Lord Asmodeus, and devils will whirl with you. |
| Zirel | And after that? |
| Demon | If my Lord is pleased with you, you will be his first. If not, he'll give you back to me. |
| Zirel | And in the morning? |
| Demon | There are no mornings there. |
| Zirel | How do we travel? |
| Demon | I will bear you on my wings to the desert. We will fly over fields of toadstools, woods of werewolves, over the ruins of Sodom where serpents are scholars, hyenas singers, whores preachers, and thieves judges. There, ugliness is beauty and mockery exaltation. But hurry for our eternity is brief. |
| Zirel | I'm afraid. |
| Demon | Everyone is … |
| Zirel | My father … |
| Demon | There are no fathers in Sodom. |
| Zirel | Tell me more about it. |

| | |
|---|---|
| Demon | Why tell? In one moment you can be there and see for yourself. |
| Zirel | And if I don't like it? |
| Demon | "If" is a bubble. Come into the mirror. |
| Zirel | What will Shloimele say? And everybody in Krashnik? Oh, my God. |
| Demon | Hurry, the night is short. |
| Zirel | Do you love me? |
| Demon | The old, old, old question! Yes, yes, yes. *Embraces her.* This did it. *Both disappear. Dark and then a dim light.* |

# Act II

# Scene 1

*Asmodeus's throne room. Asmodeus sits on a golden throne and rests his feet on a golden stool. His prime minister, Adalia, stands before him wearing a long coat and gold slippers. Naamah, a lady in waiting, fans the king with an ostrich tail.*

| | |
|---|---|
| Asmodeus | Well, what else? |
| Adalia | As I told his majesty, the situation is worse from day to day. In the big cities they don't need us at all. People are persuaded to sin through literature, theater, and so-called science—psychology, sociology, and whatever other names they have. In the villages there are still a few pious people, and from time to time one of our hobgoblins succeeds in persuading them to sin. But these are misdemeanors... |
| Asmodeus | For example... |
| Adalia | In Izhbitza, a Hebrew teacher ate a plum with worms. In Gorshkov, one of our little devils made an old man steal |

|  |  |
|---|---|
|  | his friend's snuff box. In Krasnistaw, a Yeshiva boy peeped through the hole of the women's ritual bath and— |
| Asmodeus | How about murder, rape, robbery, theft? |
| Adalia | The gentile demons have many murderers and rapists, but Jewish demons only have shopkeepers, and all they can make them do is overcharge their customers a penny, give false weight, and other such transgressions. We have plenty of thieves in our little towns, but there's little to steal. The poverty in Poland and Lithuania has reached a degree where— |
| Admodeous | How about the Jews in western Europe? |
| Adalia | They have no need of demons. They are almost all freethinkers. Some go to their fancy synagogues on Rosh Hashanah and Yom Kippur, but in these synagogues they have female choirs, and instead of repenting, the worshippers lust for the females. |
| Asmodeus | *Suddenly.* Someone's blowing the ram's horn. Is it already the month of Elul? Can you hear it? |
| Adalia | A young man by the name of Shloimele lives in Krashnik and he wants to bring the Messiah. He blows the ram's horn regularly. He's fasting and makes use of the holy names of the Kabbalah in order to frighten us and— |

| | |
|---|---|
| Asmodeus | What do we do to stop it? |
| Adalia | He has a wife, Zirel, and Hurmizah, one of ours, is making love to her. |
| Asmodeus | How can this help us? Shloimele himself should be seduced by some of our females. |
| Naamah | If my king and lord will permit me, I will go to Krashnik and defile him so that he will forget the Messiah. No male can withstand my charm, as you well know. |
| Asmodeus | Stay where you are. Wait for orders. |
| Adalia | His wife Zirel is beautiful, but he seldom approaches her, not even during her clean days. |
| Naamah | He would approach me immediately. One look from me and he would burn like fire from Gehenna. |
| Asmodeus | Better chase away the flies. You think you're eighteen. The truth is that my castle is an old age home—old he-demons, old she-demons. Our young demons have abandoned us for the gentiles or left for revolutionary Gomorrah. |
| Adalia | If his majesty isn't happy with my government, I am ready to resign. |
| Asmodeus | And who will take your place? Our whole system is falling to pieces. |
| Adalia | Believe me, my majesty, in Gomorrah things are a lot worse. In our democratic |

|  | Sodom, at least demons get enough to eat. Since the revolution, there's starvation in Gomorrah. You pay ten shekels for a measure of keebebe. Moon juice is not to be gotten at all. The price of turkey semen is outrageous. |
|---|---|
| Asmodeus | At least they have a young generation, while our she-demons haven't given birth for over fifty years. |
| Adalia | The birth rate in Gomorrah has dropped, too. A third of the male population is in prison, another third is in the army. Many are in concentration camps for all kinds of deviations and— |
| Asmodeus | Gomorrah's not for me to worry about, but for Sodom *I'm* responsible. If the Almighty should decide to bring the Messiah, we will all be wiped out. |
| Adalia | That Shloimele from Krashnik can't bring the Messiah just by blowing the ram's horn. His talismans are as strong as toilet paper. His conjurings are amateurish. Besides, if his wife leaves him, he will do what Onan did, and then— |
| Naamah | With his majesty's consent, I will leave for Krashnik and try to— |
| Asmodeus | You won't get any consent. I know all your charms. Our Sodomites have learned nothing. This is the bitter truth. |

| | |
|---|---|
| Naamah | Do I get a chance? Three hundred years ago, when I first came to this castle, I bloomed like a rose. Your great-great grandfather, Asmodeus the 72nd, looked at me once and was so enraptured that— |
| Asmodeus | I've heard this story a thousand times. The story itself has a white beard. |

*The door opens and a watchman let in Hurmizah. He's leading Zirel by a rope.*

| | |
|---|---|
| Watchmen | *To both:* Prostrate yourselves seven times before the King. |
| Asmodeus | Who are they? |
| Adalia | This is Hurmizah and the female is the wife of that Shloimele I just mentioned. Her name is Zirel. |
| Hurmizah | My king, prime minister, lady in waiting—I announce with respect that I accomplished my mission. Zirel has crossed the mirror. |
| Asmodeus | Crossed the mirror? |
| Naamah | I can't believe it. |
| Adalia | It's been at least forty years since something like that has happened. |
| Asmodeus | Bring her closer. I want to see her. Closer! My eyes are not what they used to be. |
| Naamah | I told your majesty that you need glasses. |

| | |
|---|---|
| Asmodeus | A demon with glasses—nonsense! Well, I can see her now. *To Zirel.* How old are you, woman? |
| Zirel | Twenty four. |
| Asmodeus | That's all? Here the youngest Primadonna is well over one hundred. What made you cross the mirror? |
| Zirel | I was bored. I can't stand the emptiness. The days were all alike and the nights are long and terrifying. |
| Asmodeus | How about your husband, Shloimele? Does he ignore you? |
| Zirel | For two weeks after my period I wasn't kosher, and when he finally visited me, he told me so many pious tales that I lost my desire. Hurmizah promised to marry me. |
| Naamah | Marry you? *Laughs wildly.* |
| Zirel | What's she laughing about? |
| Asmodeus | Don't laugh, Naamah. Among the humans the institution of marriage has not yet been completely liquidated. |
| Adalia | Hurmizah, now you can tell her the truth. |
| Hurmizah | The truth? I've already forgotten that such a thing exists. |
| Adalia | First of all, he's not a man. Secondly, he already has six wives. Thirdly, he's seldom in Sodom as he's sent out regularly to seduce women. |

| | |
|---|---|
| Zirel | *To Hurmizah.* Is this a fact? |
| Hurmizah | You heard what our prime minister said. |
| Zirel | *To Hurmizah.* You don't love me? |
| Naamah | *Mimics her.* Love me? *Again she bursts out laughing.* |
| Adalia | The word has become obsolete. You can't even find it in the dictionaries anymore. |
| Zirel | *To Hurmizah.* You deceived me? |
| Hurmizah | I'm a deceiver. This is my profession. *Exits.* |
| Zirel | What am I going to do now? *She cries bitterly.* |
| Asmodeus | Don't cry, woman. True, we are demons, but we are Jewish. We won't do you too much harm. In olden times, Sodom was a metropolis. In Poland, in Lithuania, in Galicia there were many saints, half-saints, quarter-saints, and our job was to lead them to sin. Their sins were our bread and our wine. Now the world has become enlightened. No one even believes in our existence. The enlightened ones sin all the time, but we no longer get credit for their sins. This is why— |
| Naamah | Forgive me, your majesty. You don't have to tell our secrets to this wench. |
| Asmodeus | I wanted her to know that Sodom is no longer what it used to be. |

| | |
|---|---|
| Zirel | The way Hurmizah described Sodom, I thought it was the happiest place in the universe. |
| Adalia | It was once. |
| Zirel | What's left for me? Can I go back home? |
| Adalia | There's no going back for those who cross the mirror. |
| Asmodeus | *To Zirel.* Are you ready to become the seventh wife of a eunuch? |
| Zirel | The seventh of a eunuch? *Laughs, then weeps.* |
| Asmodeus | Would everyone please leave my room, I want to be alone with Zirel. |
| Naamah | *Smiles, winks, and whispers so that Asmodeus doesn't hear.* He's still trying. |

*Everyone exits.*

| | |
|---|---|
| Asmodeus | Don't cry, girl, we are as I told you, Jewish demons, and we have a little heart. *Pause.* When a woman crosses the mirror, I have first rights. In olden times, these things happened often. Lately, it has become a rarity. Just the same, we believe in tradition. Be so good and get undressed. I want to see your body. |
| Zirel | King! |
| Asmodeus | No reason to be shy. I've seen more naked females than you have hair on your head. |

Zirel        Hurmizah told me that—I mean I thought that—

Asmodeus     All trouble comes from thinking. So it is with humans and so with demons. Take everything off.

Zirel        *Weeping.* Well ... *Takes off her clothes.*

Asmodeus     *Looks her over.* The daughters of Eve are still beautiful. *Long pause.* Here in Sodom, we have all become old and sick. Let me spell it out for you. We are all quite impotent. I have a large harem of wives and concubines, but none of them is able to arouse me. Do you understand me?

*Zirel nods.*

Asmodeus     For me to be able to do anything with a female, I need something special. A new approach, a new form of excitement, new inspiration. I'm like King David, who, when he got old and cold, was brought the Shunamite maiden, Abishag, who lay next to him and—

Zirel        What do I, a woman from Krashnik, know? I learned little about such things. All I know was that I was miserable and therefore—

Asmodeus     It just so happens that women of your kind have the most uncommon whims. Come closer. Sit on my lap.

| | |
|---|---|
| Zirel | No, no. |
| Asmodeus | I've neither the strength nor the patience to plead with you. If you won't do as I ask, you will be sent to pluck feathers in the kitchen, and you will never see my face again. |
| Zirel | What shall I do? |
| Asmodeus | I told you. Sit on my lap. |
| Zirel | Well ... *Sits on his lap.* |
| Asmodeus | Now say something. |
| Zirel | What shall I say? |
| Asmodeus | Something hot, fiery, something that ignites the blood and— |
| Zirel | I don't know what to say. |
| Asmodeus | Didn't you ever play with your husband? |
| Zirel | He refused. |
| Asmodeus | Have you ever desired another man besides your Shloimele? |
| Zirel | Hurmizah. |
| Asmodeus | No one else? |
| Zirel | No one else. |
| Asmodeus | Perhaps your father? |
| Zirel | My father? God forbid. |
| Asmodeus | Not even deep, deep down in your heart? |
| Zirel | Who desires one's own father? Never. |
| Asmodeus | Did you lust after another female? |
| Zirel | *Frightened.* What? |
| Asmodeus | You never heard of such things? |
| Zirel | Never. |

| | |
|---|---|
| Asmodeus | *To himself:* You have to teach her the alphabet. *To her:* Did you ever dream of becoming a harlot? |
| Zirel | A harlot? No. I thought that Hurmizah would be with me and love me and— |
| Asmodeus | We of the old generation still know what love is, but I'm afraid he has never heard of such things. He was taught a few phrases, and he repeats them like a parrot. |
| Zirel | What am I going to do? There must be some place for me in this fool's madhouse. |

*Lilith enters.*

| | |
|---|---|
| Asmodeus | I told you not to disturb me. |
| Lilith | *Pointing at Zirel.* She won't help you. *To Zirel* Get off his lap, Krashnik yokel. If not, I'll skin you alive. *Zirel gets off.* |
| Asmodeus | How dare you? You shikse! |
| Lilith | I have news for you. There's a revolution in Zvoim. |
| Asmodeus | In Zvoim too? What do they want in Zvoim? |
| Lilith | What they want everywhere: starvation, torture, murder, and fiery speeches to boot. |
| Asmodeus | The demons have gone crazy. Where's Adalia? *Calling out.* Adalia, |

|          | Adalia!*Adalia enters.* Did you hear the news about Zvoim? |
|----------|------------------------------------------------------------|
| Adalia   | Yes, my lord, just this instant.                           |
| Asmodeus | Call an immediate emergency meeting.                       |
| Adalia   | Emergency-shmergency! Who is there to call? Androgenes thinks he's King Solomon. Mamrei writes poetry. Meturaf ran away to Ethiopia with his wife's lover. There's one normal demon in the cabinet, but he sides with the rebels. |
| Asmodeus | The generals—                                              |
| Adalia   | Fast asleep after their opium party.                       |
| Lilith   | And you call yourself a prime minister?                    |
| Adalia   | I'm no longer eager for the honor. *Removes medal from around his throat and hands it to Lilith.* I'm going. |
| Asmodeus | Don't run. Don't run. This is not the time to abandon the ship. |
| Lilith   | As a rule, this is what rats do.                           |
| Adalia   | My skin is more valuable to me than all the Sodom hypocrisy. *Makes a move to run out.* |
| Lilith   | He's right, too. Where are you going, Adalia? |
| Adalia   | While it's still dark, maybe I can cross the border to Admah. |
| Lilith   | Wait. I'll go with you.                                    |
| Adalia   | Make it fast. *Both leave.*                                |
| Asmodeus | It seems like the end of our democratic monarchy. *To Zirel.* You have chosen the |

wrong time to cross the mirror. Had
you come fifty or a hundred years ago,
we would have known what to do with
you. Now it's too late in every respect.
*Pause.* Though we are demons, we want
law and order to reign, but the young
generation doesn't want any rest.

Zirel    May I get dressed?

Asmodeus    You might as well. *Long pause.* There
is a God, there is. The angels advised
him not to create man and his counter-
part, the demon. But he didn't listen.
He wanted to bestow on humanity the
greatest gift he has to offer: free choice.
But they crave to be like cattle, beasts,
flies, rocks—both men and demons.

Zirel    What will happen to us?

Asmodeus    *Laughs.* Us? I'll be tortured by revolu-
tionaries. For you they will find some
use. Even the fallen angels loved the
daughter of man. *Leans his head on the
chair and falls asleep.*

*Curtain*

# SCENE 2

*Late at night. Asmodeus cannot sleep and Zirel is reading aloud to him from a storybook.*

Zirel   When God ordained the Flood in the time of Noah, the demons came to the Ark together with the animals and fowl, wanting to be saved. But Noah forbade them to enter. However, Noah liked to drink, and when he was asleep his son, Ham, allowed a single pair to enter, and all the demons on the surface of the earth are descend from them. Those who could not enter the Ark found a cave that led to a labyrinth 350 miles deep, and there they saved themselves. Their leader, Mumar, sealed the opening with a huge rock. They have remained there since and have created a colony in the netherworld. They no longer need to persuade men to sin. Even God has no power over them.

|          | They established their own kingdom and— |
|----------|-----------------------------------------|
| Asmodeus | *Yawns.* How I envy them! How I wish I could hide myself in a cave—far from humana and demons alike. If in addition I could find the right kind of female there, perhaps my powers might return to me. |
| Zirel    | Shall I continue to read? |
| Asmodeus | Yes, do. *Falls asleep.* |

*Hurmizah enters.*

|          |                                         |
|----------|-----------------------------------------|
| Zirel    | Hurmizah! |
| Hurmizah | I was looking for you all over the palace. |
| Zirel    | More lies? You ugly seducer! |
| Hurmizah | No, Zirel. In a situation like this, even a demon does not lie. |
| Zirel    | What's the truth? |
| Hurmizah | For the first time in all my memory, love has awakened in me. For you, Zirel, for you. |
| Zirel    | If you love me, help me to go home. |
| Hurmizah | Throughout history, no one has crossed the mirror twice. As far as I can see, both man's kingdom and the kingdom of the demons are coming to an end. God wanted to create another God—man—and he lost his power altogether. |

| | |
|---|---|
| Zirel | Who's in power now? Tell me! |
| Hurmizah | The cold ether, the stiff laws. |
| Zirel | Who made the laws? |
| Hurmizah | They've always existed—blind giants sunk in eternal sleep. |

*The blowing of a ram's horn is heard.*

| | |
|---|---|
| Zirel | The ram's horn, here, in the lowest abyss? |
| Hurmizah | Your husband is summoning the idol of mercy. |
| Zirel | An idol? Can there be a God without mercy? |
| Hurmizah | The true God is a God of wrath. |
| Zirel | Take me to the idol of mercy. I want to prostrate myself before him. I want to die at his feet. |
| Hurmizah | He has no substance. The Jews invented him—a God who was supposed to defend the poor, the weak, the downtrodden. A God who's on the side of the sheep, not the wolf. There isn't such an entity. The true God is not even on the side of the wolf. |
| Zirel | Whose side is he on? |
| Hurmizah | On the side of hunger and shame. |
| Zirel | I wanted to hide from him. That's the reason I'm here. |
| Hurmizah | He is even more evil than we are. He is the Arch-Demon. |

Zirel          Is there no salvation anywhere?

*Steps and voices are heard.*

Hurmizah      Someone's coming. Let's hide.

*They disappear behind a side door. Adalia, Lilith, Naamah enter.*

Lilith         He's sleeping, the old fool. Look at the great Asmodeus. Asleep with a crown on his silly head.
Naamah         That head will soon be chopped off.
Lilith         I'll take the crown. *Removes the crown from Asmodeus' head.*
Adalia         Yes, it might be useful. The rebels in Zvoim will need lots of gold to sustain the revolution.
Lilith         What else can we steal?
Adalia         Somewhere he's supposed to have the constitution of Sodom, written on parchment. It would be a precious gift to bring to his enemies.
Lilith         Where is this stupid constitution?
Naamah         If I'm not mistaken, it's hidden somewhere in his throne.
Adalia         Find it. We can't come to Zvoim empty-handed.
Naamah         He may wake up.
Lilith         And what if he does? A deposed king is worth less than a dead bat.

| | |
|---|---|
| Naamah | *Searching the throne and removing a parchment.* Here it is. |
| Adalia | Give it to me. *Reads.* We, the demons, who call ourselves the sons of Eve, the children of Keturah, the lords of Esau, gathered together in the city of Sodom to bring order to our conduct so that our lives should not be constantly threatened, so that our children should have a home, and so our wives and concubines can find protection and—*Laughs.* |
| Lilith | The dreams of a Jewish demon. |
| Naamah | Were the Ten Commandments any smarter? |
| Adalia | *Pointing at Asmodeus.* I've never seen him sleep so deeply. |
| Lilith | And to think that I once loved this creature. |
| Naamah | A single word from him set my blood on fire. |
| Lilith | His touch made me hot and wet. Now— |

*Lilith and Naamah kiss each other passionately.*

| | |
|---|---|
| Adalia | There will be enough time for that. Let's go while it's still night. |

*All three exit. Asmodeus awakens.*

| | |
|---|---|
| Asmodeus | G on, Zirel, go on. *Suddenly:* Where is she, that daughter of man? *Reaching for* |

*his crown.* My crown! Stolen! Adalia!
Where's Adalia? Naamah! Guards!

*Hurmizah and Zirel return.*

| | |
|---|---|
| Asmodeus | Here she is. What did you do with my crown, you thief from Krashnik? |
| Hurmizah | My Lord, Lilith took your crown. |
| Asmodeus | Lilith? |
| Hurmizah | And Naamah stole the constitution from under your throne. |
| Asmodeus | What for? |
| Hurmizah | They intend to surrender to the enemy. |
| Asmodeus | What enemy? I have so many enemies that I no longer remember who is who. |
| Hurmizah | They're defecting to Zvoim. |
| Asmodeus | Only a week ago their king and I signed an agreement ... |
| Hurmizah | His head is already being chopped off. |
| Asmodeus | Did they also take the storybook? |
| Zirel | Here, my king, is the storybook. |
| Asmodeus | *To Zirel.* My advice is—leave. Any minute the rebels may come and destroy everything. Why should you suffer for my mistakes? |
| Zirel | I haven't any place to go, my Lord. |
| Asmodeus | *To Hurmizah.* Why did you bring her at a time like this? |
| Hurmizah | I was given orders and I went. I'm still nothing but a royal errand boy. |

| | |
|---|---|
| Asmodeus | Do the members of my staff know what they're doing? Mice and grasshoppers are smarter than they are. They were trapped in the spider web of routine and were never able to free themselves. My only comfort is that the same thing will happen in Zvoim. *To Zirel.* What's is happening among the humans? |
| Zirel | Krashnik is neither human nor demonic. No yoke was put on my shoulders. I broke down because of a lack of burdens. |
| Asmodeus | *To Hurmizah.* Take her and go some-place with her. Since you are half human, perhaps you two will be able to copulate. Where are your other wives? |
| Zirel | Yes, where *are* they? |
| Hurmizah | They forsook me long ago and lie with each other. |
| Asmodeus | The same thing occurred before the Flood. *Pause.* Without my crown, my head feels cold. *Laughs.* |
| Zirel | Shall I find a hat for my Lord? |
| Asmodeus | By the time you find a hat, there will be no head for it. |
| Zirel | *After some hesitation.* Perhaps all three of us can go away together. |
| Hurmizah | How many times should I tell you that there is no way back through the mirror. |
| Zirel | Perhaps we can remain inside the mirror. |

| | |
|---|---|
| Hurmizah | A mirror is made to appear and disappear. Those who dwell in the mirror become blind, or even worse, insane. |
| Asmodeus | Can one make love in the mirror? |
| Hurmizah | Where there is no depth there is no penetration. |
| Asmodeus | Since you have been a mirror man all your life, can one sleep in a mirror. |
| Hurmizah | I never tried. |
| Zirel | Since the depth is being destroyed, perhaps the surface will acquire a substance. I always envied the things in the mirror, though my mother warned me that looking too much in the mirror will end in disaster. |
| Asmodeus | As I'm doomed anyhow, I could just as well die in the mirror as in the torture house of Zvoim. |
| Hurmizah | Can you still fly, my Lord? |
| Asmodeus | I haven't flown for a long time. I even forgot that we possess the power of the insects. But we can try. |
| Hurmizah | If you want to fly, my Lord, we should do it now. You, Zirel, will sit on my shoulders. *To Asmodeus.* Is there anything, my Lord, you want to take with you? |
| Asmodeus | Since my life has become nothing but a story, the storybook is the only possession I will take. |
| Hurmizah | *To himself.* Just now, in the midst of all this turmoil, when everything is |

|            | collapsing, the worst of all sicknesses has befallen me—love. |
|------------|---------------------------------------------------------------|
| Zirel      | So you deceived yourself as well as me.                       |
| Hurmizah   | With us, all truths become lies, and lies sometimes become truths—against our will. |
| Asmdeous   | This is what love is. It jumps on you like a vampire. If you fight, it bites, and if you surrender, it sucks your blood. |
| Hurmizah   | You sill remember these things, my king?                      |
| Asmodeus   | It's the last thing a demon will forget.                      |

*Curtain*

# SCENE 3

*Takes place inside the mirror (whatever that means). Asmodeus is asleep in his chair.*

Hurmizah   We're alone, Zirel. Our Lord is fast asleep. Our privacy is absolute. We are not being reflected in a single mirror throughout the entire universe. Even God, the mirror of all mirrors, cannot see us.

Zirel   What do you want, Hurmizah? I told you that I could not love you.

Hurmizah   You loved me when you followed me across the mirror.

Zirel   Only for a moment. *Pause.* You don't need any love, Hurmizah. You know it yourself.

Hurmizah   What do I need?

Zirel   To tease, to tickle—to invoke a hunger that you cannot satisfy, neither in yourself nor in another.

Hurmizah   I beg you, Zirel, kiss me, embrace me.

Zirel   Woe to the love that begs. *Embraces him.*

Hurmizah *Kisses her.* What a punishment, always to look at the food that you cannot taste.

Zirel The demons talk too much. This is their misfortune.

Hurmizah What is talk? Mirrors of deeds. And what are deeds? Mirrors of thoughts. Love too is a mirror—it's all surface. *Gives her a long, drawn kiss.*

Zirel Hurmizah, enough.

Hurmizah I want you.

Zirel You want to want.

Hurmizah Spit on me. Perhaps this will help.

Zirel It won't help. *Spits on him.*

Hurmizah Step on me. Straddle my back, ride me like a horse. Grab my hair as you would a horse's reins. *He gets down on the floor on all fours.*

Zirel Oh, you make me meshuggah. *Does as he tells her.*

*Asmodeus awakens, looks around confused.*

Asmodeus At it again? It won't help, Hurmizah. *Hurmizah and Zirel get up. Asmodeus yawns.* Who would ever expect the great Asmodeus to end up in a Krashnik mirror?

Hurmizah Your great, great, great grandfather, Asmodeus III, cast King Solomon four hundred miles from his home.

|  | He walked around and kept announcing, "I am King Solomon," but no one believed him. Now, my Lord, your time has come. |
| Asmodeus | Solomon finally returned to Jerusalem. But my throne was taken over by rebels from Zvoim. *Pause.* What do they want, these demons? When they are enslaved, they scream for freedom. When they get freedom, they want slavery. What do they need freedom for when they all follow the herd. What they really crave for is permanent rebellion. *To Zirel.* Read me stories that some anonymous Kabbalist has composed during sleepless nights in a bed without love. |
| Zirel | Again a story? |
| Asmodeus | What is the world if not a story? Time, like the tides, obliterates all things and nothing remains but a story in mirror writing. |
| Hurmizah | When, my Lord, did the story begin? |
| Asmodeus | The story of the world has no beginning. Therein lies its perplexing charm. |
| Hurmizah | Will it at least have an end? |
| Asmodeus | Regretfully, not even this. |
| Zirel | *Opens a book and reads aloud.* Once there was— |
| Asmodeus | What was there once? |
| Zirel | A God who lived through innumerable eternities. He did nothing and he had |

|  | nothing to do. He had everything in himself: the Crown, the Wisdom, the Understanding, the Mercy, the Strength, the Beauty, the Everlastingness, the Glamour, the Fundamentality, the Kingship. |
|---|---|
| Asmodeus | He was both the mirror and the image? |
| Zirel | Suddenly he was taken by a desire to create. |
| Asmodeus | Suddenly? Wasn't creativity one of His attributes? |
| Zirel | *Continues to read.* But where was there room for creation when God filled all space? |
| Hurmizah | So what did he do? |
| Zirel | He shrunk himself and created a void in himself. Without a void, creation is impossible. |
| Hurmizah | How can God lessen himself? Isn't that a contradiction? |
| Asmodeus | The omnipotent must be able to do anything—even to make faces before a mirror. |
| Zirel | *Reads.* The void that he created was dark and— |
| Hurmizah | How could the void be dark if God's light radiated from all sides? |
| Asmodeus | The Almighty must be able to extinguish his lamps. |

| | |
|---|---|
| Zirel | *Reads.* That darkness became the canvas and the background on which God painted his picture. |
| Hurmizah | He's a painter, not a storyteller? |
| Asmodeus | Kitsch paintings tell a story. |
| Hurmizah | What did he paint? |
| Zirel | *Reads.* Myriads of mirrors, concave and convex, that reflected angels, seraphim, cherubs, holy animals. Then he painted humanity. |
| Hurmizah | A self-portrait? |
| Asmodeus | A caricature of himself. *Again falls asleep.* |

*The living room in Krashnik is seen again. Shloimele enters without a coat, in his fringed garment, with a skullcap on his head. He carries a book and a ram's horn.*

| | |
|---|---|
| Shloimele | Where are you, Zirel? Where are you? Zirel, daughter of Abraham, I implore you, return to your husband! I yearn for you day and night. My longing consumes me. I cannot even concentrate on my prayers. |
| Zirel | He really loved me. |
| Shloimele | No one can disappear completely. |
| Zirel | I'm here, Shloimele, in the mirror. |
| Hurmizah | *To Zirel.* He can't hear you. Don't waste your breath. |
| Zirel | But he's so close. This was our room. |

| | |
|---|---|
| Hurmizah | The same room, but another dimension. The time too, is different. |
| Shloimele | *Perks his ears.* Do you hear me, Zirel? If you do, I implore you, answer me. |
| Zirel | I hear you, Shloimele. |
| Shloimele | Have you become silent forever? Will I never hear your sweet voice again? |
| Zirel | He never spoke this way before. |
| Hurmizah | It often happens that love awakens when there is no longer any one to love. |
| Shloimele | I sinned against you, Zirel. I wanted to redeem the world and I forgot those who were near me and who waited for my word, my friendship, my kindness. I left you alone when I should have been close to you. |
| Zirel | This realization came too late, Shloimele. |
| Shloimele | I regret it, Zirel. |
| Zirel | You must find comfort without me. |
| Shloimele | If the Torah does not help me, what comfort can I find? I'm tortured by one thought: Will we ever meet again or are we doomed to eternal separation? |
| Zirel | One day we will meet again. |
| Shloimele | Where? |
| Hurmizah | Do you really miss him? |
| Zirel | For the first time, yes. |
| Hurmizah | Shall I bring him into the mirror? Are you willing to be shared by the two of us? |

Zirel        If you can do it, bring him over.

Hurmizah     If I cannot have you alone, perhaps sharing will help.

Shloimele    I can't hear your voice, Zirel, but I feel your presence.

*Hurmizah appears in the mirror. Shloimele sees him and trembles/*

Shloimele    *Screaming.* Shaddai—destroy Satan!

Hurmizah     Don't try to frighten me with your Kabbalah. If you want your Zirel, come to me into the mirror.

Shloimele    Who are you? A devil, a goblin, Shabriri? Briri? *Blows ram's horn.* Give my wife back to me, or—

Hurmizah     There can be no talk of giving back, but if you want to share her with me, we can do business.

Shloimele    Share? With a demon? God forbid. In the name of the Angels Gabriel, Raphael, Uriel—

Hurmizah     He still thinks he has the upper hand.

Shloimele    *Looks around and around, bewildered.* Shema Israel!

*The Jew of Babylon enters.*

Reb Yoyets   Shloimele, why are you screaming?

Shloimele    I saw him.

Reb Yoyets   Who?

| | |
|---|---|
| Shloimele | The unclean one, the destroyer, Ketev-Mereri. |
| Reb Yoyets | Where? |
| Shloimele | In the mirror. |
| Reb Yoyets | *Looks into the mirror.* The evil host is there. |
| Shloimele | The evil one wanted to share her with me. He's supposed to be her man. *Spits.* |
| Reb Yoyets | Through you he hopes to gain his manhood. Sharing was always the devil's sport. |
| Shloimele | It's all my fault. All her sins fall on my head. *Weeps and exits.* |
| Reb Yoyets | *To himself.* My time is up. All my ambitions have evaporated. My friends are no longer friends, and even my enemies are not enemies any more. Just the same, I have a feeling that I haven't lived at all. Each day I sacrificed for tomorrow, and all the tomorrows became yesterdays. Where are you hiding, yesterdays? In what devilish mirror? Well, everything's lost. *Exits.* |
| Zirel | I destroyed him too. |
| Asmodeus | *Awakens and points with his finger towards the Jew of Babylon.* A demon who lived all his years among humans and waged war on us. |
| Zirel | You know him, my Lord? |
| Asmodeus | I used to know all my subjects. |
| Zirel | Perhaps I, too, am one of yours. |

| Asmodeus | There are those who belong neither to humankind nor to the devil. |
| Zirel | What are they? |
| Asmodeus | Eternal misfits. God's mistakes. The shavings of creation. |
| Zirel | Is there no place for us at all? |
| Asmodeus | Somewhere in infinity there must be a place for everyone. Behind God's canvas mistakes are no mistakes, sins are no sins, and grief is no grief. There must be an answer to all questions, but where it is, no one knows, not even my boss. *Points towards Heaven.* |
| Zirel | The answer is death. |
| Asmodeus | Death is nothing more than a corridor between two hells. |
| Zirel | I mean absolute death—sleep without any awakening and without dreams. This sleep preceded God and may outlast him. I feel it's coming. It is my only love. |
| Hurmizah | Don't leave me Zirel. Only now am I beginning to really see your image. |
| Zirel | I have to go. I played my play and danced my dance. My final bridegroom is waiting for me. Once united, we will never part again. *Disappears.* |
| Hurmizah | *Cries out:* Zirel! |
| Asmodeus | She's gone. Above all surfaces. Above all mirrors. Where all difference ceases. Where God is Asmodeus and |

|            | Asmodeus is God, and both together are an abyss of forgetfulness. |
| Hurmizah   | Without her there's no sense in our remaining here. |
| Asmodeus   | A mirror is an inn, not a home. |
| Hurmizah   | Where is home? |
| Asmodeus   | Of all illusions in the various mirrors, home is the greatest. |
| Hurmizah   | In Sodom the revolution will decimate us. |
| Asmodeus   | Me, not you. |
| Hurmizah   | In that case, remain here, my Lord. |
| Asmodeus   | Alone in a mirror? Too lonesome a place even for an old demon. In Sodom, at least they'll put me on trial. My wives will bear witness against me. My friends will spit on me. The executioner will torture me— |
| Hurmizah   | And then? |
| Asmodeus   | Then the page will be turned over and I will become a bedtime story for children. An exciting tale for grownups and a tale of horror for the old. |

*Shloimele appears again.*

| Shloimele  | Zirel, where are you? |
| Hurmizah   | *Mimics him.* Zirel where are you? We're both widowers of the same wife. |
| Asmodeus   | *Points to Shloimele.* He too is needed. He is also part of the story. |

| | |
|---|---|
| Hurmizah | *To Asmodeus.* I will long for her as long as I live. |
| Asmodeus | In the beginning there was longing. God yearned and he didn't know for what. Therefore he created the system of mirrors, which is called the universe,all surface, all distortion, all deception. |
| Hurmizah | Are you ready to go with me, my Lord? |
| Asmodeus | Yes, the rooster will soon crow. |

*They embrace and shake in demonic love scene.*

# Scene 4

*The same evening. The Jew of Babylon sits alone in Zirel's boudoir, dozing. He opens his eyes.*

Reb Yoyets    *He listens.* They're sleeping. Happy are those who sleep.

*A she-demon appears in the mirror.*

Reb Yoyets    *Frightened, beginning to recite an incantation:*

> Run away to the Black Mountains,
> Beneath a black sky,
> Where birds won't fly and snakes won't crawl—

She-Demon    *Laughs.* Don't you recognize me?
Reb Yoyets    Who are you? What do you want?
She-Demon    How old you are! Oh, what the years do to the human clan.
Reb Yoyets    Who are you?
She-Demon    Take a good look.

Reb Yoyets    I have only one good eye and at night even this is bad.

She-Demon    Batnaamah.

Reb Yoyets    *Exclaims.* Batnaamah!

She-Demon    So you still remember me?

Reb Yoyets    How can one forget you?

She-Demon    I tried to appear to you many times, but you are covered with so many talismans that I never had a chance.

Reb Yoyets    You look just like you looked the last time I saw you. No change whatsoever.

She-Demon    This is what all men say. But in a way it's true. The years don't ravage us as they do your kind.

Reb Yoyets    You've even become more beautiful.

She-Demon    Perhaps riper.

Reb Yoyets    What are you doing? Where are you?

She-Demon    There's much to tell. I'm still in the netherworld.

Reb Yoyets    Did you get married?

She-Demon    I got married and divorced. Married again and divorced again.

Reb Yoyets    And now?

She-Demon    It's about ten years now that I stopped making a fool of myself with marriages.

Reb Yoyets    Where are you? In Sodom?

She-Demon    Not exactly Sodom, but in that region.

Reb Yoyets    Where, in Zoar?

She-Demon    Between Admah and Zevoim.

Reb Yoyets    Well, so …

She-Demon     I never forgot you, Yoyetz. There were times when I was consumed with passion for others, but my love for you never diminished.

Reb Yoyets    There's not a day when I don't think about you.

She-Demon     I know everything, all your doings. Many times I sat in your chimney and listened to your talk. Really, Yoyetz, I don't understand you.

Reb Yoyets    I no longer understand myself.

She-Demon     What is the reason for the war you keep waging with us? It would make sense if you were a holy man, but basically you are one of us. Why fight us all the time?

Reb Yoyets    You know why. For money. My life had to have some purpose.

She-Demon     What have you accomplished with all your money? No home, no child. You are a broken shard. I know all your females. The whole lot of them. Forgive me for saying so, but not one of them was right for you. There was not a single one among them who could give you a thousandth part of the pleasure I gave you.

Reb Yoyets    It's true, Batnaamah, but you returned to them while I remained among the humans. I couldn't be satisfied only with memories.

She-Demons What are doing here in the middle of the night? Why are you sitting on a chair instead of lying in bed? A man your age should rest at night.

Reb Yoyets A female from this house vanished. She entered this very mirror and is gone.

She-Demon Mirrors are open graves. But women have such a passion for looking at themselves, that no danger can restrain them.

Reb Yoyets Would you have any idea where this particular woman might be? Her name is Zirel, the daughter of Abraham and Temerl.

She-Demon How can I know about every wench who falls into our hands? I seldom listen to gossip. I've isolated myself completely.

Reb Yoyets From men too?

She-Demon From everybody.

Reb Yoyets Why?

She-Demon Demons keep talking about love, but when it comes to the real thing, they don't know what it's all about. It's hate, not love. First, they're half crazy. Second, they suffer from all sorts of inhibitions. Though they themselves are not competent, they demand the most perfect performance from the female.

Reb Yoyets The demons too?

| | |
|---|---|
| She-Demon | Those with whom I have dealings are all old. The young revolutionary generation I don't understand at all. |
| Reb Yoyets | What do they want? |
| She-Demon | Just to fight. They invent all sorts of causes. They always appear in big crowds. They've overthrown Asmodeus. They made an imp into the new king. |
| Reb Yoyets | So you're all alone. |
| She-Demon | Yes, Yoyetz. I'm tired of all their empty talk. They're constantly bewailing their lot. Every third demon thinks he was born to ruin the world but never got a break. All they want is to weep on the shoulders of a she-demon. I'm happier resting all alone in my cave at night. |
| Reb Yoyets | Can you sleep? I doze off for a while and wake up immediately. |
| She-Demon | I can't sleep either. I just lie and think most of the night. |
| Reb Yoyets | What do you think about? |
| She-Demon | You don't deserve to know it, but mostly about you. After all, I've given you the best years of my life. You will never know, Yoyetz, how deeply I loved you. |
| Reb Yoyets | Nevertheless, you left me. |
| She-Demon | How could I have stayed with you, when you had a different female every night? I lay in the attic, between spiderwebs and devil's dung, while you cavorted with humans, with werewolves, with |

the lowliest creatures. If I hadn't left you, I would have died from anguish.

Reb Yoyets   The old complaints…

She-Demon   Since you didn't forget me, and I didn't forget you, why vegetate separately? Let's live out our last years together.

Reb Yoyets   In my case, it's the last days.

She-Demon   Things are not as bad as you think. All you need is rest and someone to take care of you.

Reb Yoyets   The netherworld is only waiting for me to come down to them. I heard there was a revolution in Zvoim.

She-Demon   Revolution or no revolution, demons remain demons. The old ones are senile, the young ones are crazy. Everything is as it should be.

Reb Yoyets   It's too late, Batnaamah. Too late for everything.

She-Demon   Believe me, Yoyetz, it wasn't easy for me to find you. *Suddenly, with vigor:* I won't let you get away from me in the condition you're in! Listen to me. Come over to me, into the mirror. I have a soft bed for you. I have countless stories to tell you—stories that can revive the dead.

Reb Yoyets   Things that happened to you?

She-Demon   To me, to others. You know how things are tied and connected to each other.

Reb Yoyets   Who knows how many demons you fornicated with all these years.

| | |
|---|---|
| She-Demon | Not as many as you think. I'm not one of those who fall in love easily. Propositions I got many, but I have to love a demon before I surrender to him. |
| Reb Yoyets | How many did you lie with? A thousand? |
| She-Demon | Much less. |
| Reb Yoyets | What will happen to my house? What will I do with my gold? |
| She-Demon | Your house is a ruin and you don't need your gold there. Sins are legal tender with us, and you have a sizeable account in our banks. With interest, too. |
| Reb Yoyets | Are you sure you have no one? |
| She-Demon | Almost no one. |
| Reb Yoyets | Almost? |
| She-Demon | There is still one old demon who's attached to me, but the moment you arrive, I will make him go. |
| Reb Yoyets | What are the chances of finding Zirel? |
| She-Demon | Not good, but if you find her, and she's willing, I'll let you have your way. You can even bring her to my cave. The years had made me smart. |
| Reb Yoyets | At least let me make my confession. |
| She-Demon | For whom? He in the seventh heaven doesn't hear and doesn't care. |
| Reb Yoyets | I always hoped I would repent before I went. |

She-Demon   Don't utter this word. It's completely archaic.

Reb Yoyets   Well, it seems to be fated. How do you enter a mirror?

She-Demon   Give me your hand. And don't tremble. Demons love their enemies more than their friends.

Reb Yoyets   What more can I lose?

*She leads him through the mirror. Ketev Merreri appears with his company of demons.*

Adalia   You did a good job, Batnaamah. *To Yoyetz.* Let's go, traitor. *Puts his paw on Yoyetz's shoulder.*

Reb Yoyets   *To She-Demon:* So you trapped me, after all. Very clever. And I'm a mighty fool.

She-Demon   I'm sorry, Yoyetz, it's the revolution. It was my life for your life. But I love you just the same.

Reb Yoyets   Demon love.

She-Demon   Not any different from human love.

*Curtain*

# SCENE 5

| Yenta | *Yenta is reading a storybook aloud*: And when the Queen of Sheba heard of Solomon's wisdom and his riches and of the wonderful chair he built for himself, she developed a great desire to meet him and to hear his wise words. She took many slaves with her, male and female, as well as camels, donkeys, elephants and precious gifts, and traveled to Jerusalem. And when King Solomon heard that the Queen of Sheba arrived with her large retinue, he sat down on his golden chair that has twelve crystal steps— |
|---|---|

*Kileh the maid opens the door.*

| Kileh | Mistress. |
|---|---|
| Yenta | Yes, Kileh? |
| Kileh | What shall I cook for supper? |
| Yenta | Cook what you wish. |

| | |
|---|---|
| Kileh | The butchers bought an ox but they haven't slaughtered it yet. |
| Yenta | Please, let me read. |
| Kileh | Shall I have the spotted hen killed? |
| Yenta | As far as I'm concerned you can even kill the green one. |
| Kileh | Why does the mistress sit alone? They're pickling cucumbers at Pesha's. Many women will be there. The mistress was invited. |
| Yenta | I have nothing to talk to them about. |
| Kileh | When the ox is slaughtered, shall I buy a foot? |
| Yenta | A foot, a head. Buy whatever you want. |
| Kileh | As the mistress says. *She exits.* |
| Yenta | *Continues to read.* And King Solomon spoke words of great wisdom to the queen and they pleased her much, and he opened all his treasures before her and she admired them greatly. And even though King Solomon had a thousand wives and many more concubines, the queen aroused in him a desire for her— |

*Shloimele enters wearing a long coat and a pointed hat. He carries a stick in his hand and a beggar's pack on his shoulder.*

| | |
|---|---|
| Shloimele | Step-mother-in-law, I came to say good bye. |

| | |
|---|---|
| Yenta | Are you really leaving? |
| Shloimele | Yes, it's time for me to go. |
| Yenta | See what clothes he puts on. Like a man from the poorhouse. |
| Shloimele | All flesh and blood is poor. |
| Yenta | What are you carrying in this pack? Food? |
| Shloimele | Holy books. |
| Yenta | Books will not satisfy your hunger. |
| Shloimele | Bread grows on fields for all, but good books are few and for few. |
| Yenta | Where are you going, Shloimele? |
| Shloimele | To the yeshiva in Lublin. |
| Yenta | On foot? |
| Shloimele | There's no rush. |
| Yents | Perhaps I shouldn't tell you this, but you're allowed to remarry. The rabbi told me that since Zirel deserted you for the evil ones, you're like a widower. You don't even need the signature of a hundred Rabbis. |
| Shloimele | I know, but… |
| Yenta | But what? You are still a young man and have no children. |
| Shloimele | I'm going to be a recluse. |
| Yenta | Why a recluse? |
| Shloimele | Why build an abode of spider webs when one can build a marble mansion? The flesh decays but the Torah and God's commandments are eternal. |
| Yenta | So why did God create the flesh? |

| | |
|---|---|
| Shloimele | Only for temptation. |
| Yenta | Wait, I'll give you some money. |
| Shloimele | I don't need any money. |
| Yenta | I won't let you leave like this. You are my husband's former son-in-law and to me you are like my own child. |
| Shloimele | I'm very much obliged, but— |

*Abraham enters.*

| | |
|---|---|
| Abraham | So you made up your mind to leave us. |
| Shloimele | Yes, father-in-law. |
| Abraham | As I told you, I would be very happy if you would stay in my house, but if you're determined to leave, I'll give you your dowry. It's right here in the drawer. *Opens the drawer.* |
| Shloimele | Father-in-law, God should reward you for your generosity, but I don't need it. |
| Abraham | Stubborn as ever. Money is necessary, even for holy purpose. One needs money to build a yeshiva. |
| Shloimele | There's no lack of study houses in Poland, thank God. |
| Abraham | Printing books is expensive. |
| Shloimele | If only people would observe what is written in the old books, the Messiah would have come long ago. |
| Abraham | Well, I'll tell Zelig the coachman to harness the britska and take you to Lublin. |

| | |
|---|---|
| Shloimele | No, father-in-law. I intend to walk. |
| Abraham | Why walk when there are horses to take you? Really, Shloimele, one is not allowed to torture oneself. |
| Shloimele | Those who don't torture themselves often torture others. |
| Abraham | So it's torture one way or another. |
| Shloimele | I was the cause of the misfortune that befell your daughter, blessed be her memory. I'm a sinner and I must repent. |
| Yenta | There's a saying: those who sin don't repent and those who repent didn't sin. |
| Shloimele | If I had the sense never to marry, but to devote myself completely to the Torah, your daughter would be alive now. Father-in-law, I killed her. I'm a murderer and I have to atone like a murderer. |
| Yenta | No, no, no! |
| Abraham | I don't think there was a single man in all of Poland who could have made my daughter happy. Perhaps she too should have remained alone, but there isn't such a thing as a Jewish cloister. |
| Shloimele | I will pray for his sacred soul. I will study the Mishnah and say Kaddish for her. There are no lost souls. At the End of Days, every soul will be redeemed. |

|               | Good bye, father-in-law. Good bye, mother-in-law. |
|---------------|---------------------------------------------------|
| Yenta and Abraham | Good bye, God bless you! |

*Shloimele exits.*

| Yenta | *Falls on Abraham and cries.* If they had at least left you a grandchild! |
|-------|---------------------------------------------------------------------------|
| Abraham | It wasn't God's will. |
| Yenta | You should have married a young girl, not me. I'm nothing but a dried-up tree. |
| Abraham | Don't say this, Yenta. I wouldn't exchange you for anyone. |
| Yenta | Master. *Falls on her knees and grabs his legs.* |
| Abraham | What are you doing? This is forbidden. Get up! |
| Yenta | Master, I don't want you to die child-less. Divorce me. You've given me many happy days already. Half a year with you is better than seventy years with someone else. |
| Abraham | Get up! |
| Yenta | I'm willing to remain your servant. I'll raise your children. |
| Abraham | You torment me with these words. With God's help, we will sit in Paradise together after 120 years. |

| | |
|---|---|
| Yenta | Without a Kaddish they will not allow us into Paradise. |
| Abraham | With you I'm even willing to go to Gehenna. |
| Yenta | If I could only cut out my heart and give it to you as a gift, I would be the happiest woman in the world. |
| Abraham | *Raises her by force.* These are the words of pagans, not Jews. We Jews are God's slaves, but not slaves to slaves. Come, I will take you to lie down and rest. |

*He kisses her. Leads her by the hand and they both exit. For a while the stage is empty. Then Kileh enters.*

| | |
|---|---|
| Kileh | Mistress, they've slaughtered the ox. *Realizes no one is there.* Where did she go? Most probably to sleep in the middle of the day. Taken on the ways of the high born! If Temerl could see this, she would turn over in her grave. *Looks at the open book.* She's even reading, the great lady. Pish posh! *Looks into the book.* And then King Solomon said to the Queen of Sheba: "Stay here and become my queen and you will sit on my right side and all my court will bow at your feet." And the Queen of Sheba replied: "My King, I've left my people in the land of Ethiopia and I must return to them, but I would be the happiest woman if |

I could bear your son who would sit on
my throne after I die—"

*Kileh suddenly looks up and sees Hurmizah in the mirror.*

| | |
|---|---|
| Kileh | My, how ugly you are! |
| Demon | My, how beautiful *you* are! |

*End*